Betty Crocker

the big book of pasta

Houghton Mifflin Harcourt

Boston • New York • 2015

GENERAL MILLS

Owned Media & Publishing Director:
Amy Halford

Owned Media & Publishing Manager:
Audra Carson

Senior Editor: Grace Wells

Recipe Development and Testing:
Betty Crocker Kitchens

Photography: General Mills Photography
Studios and Image Library

HOUGHTON MIFFLIN HARCOURT

Publisher: Natalie Chapman

Editorial Director: Cindy Kitchel

Executive Editor: Anne Ficklen

Editorial Associate: Molly Aronica

Managing Editor: Marina Padakis

Associate Production Editor:
Helen Seachrist

Cover Design: Tai Blanche

Interior Design and Layout: Tai Blanche

Senior Production Coordinator:
Kimberly Kiefer

For information about permission to reproduce selections from this book, write to trade.permissions@hmhco.com or to Permissions, Houghton Mifflin Harcourt Publishing Company, 3 Park Avenue, 19th Floor, New York, New York 10016.

www.hmhco.com

Library of Congress Cataloging-in-Publication Data is available.

ISBN 978-0-544-57998-9 (trade paper); 978-0-544-58006-0 (ebk)

Manufactured in the United States of America

DOC 10 9 8 7 6 5 4 3 2 1

Cover photos: Bacon-Pepper Mac and Cheese (page 288), Chicken and Spinach-Stuffed Shells (page 272), Lemon Shrimp Fettuccine (page 106), Southwest Pasta Salad (page 202), Moroccan Spinach Lasagna (page 316), Spaghetti and Meatballs (page 40)

The Betty Crocker Kitchens seal guarantees success in your kitchen. Every recipe has been tested in America's Most Trusted Kitchens™ to meet our high standards of reliability, easy preparation and great taste.

FIND MORE GREAT IDEAS AT
BettyCrocker.com

Dear Friends,

We love our pasta because it is so versatile, easy to cook and ideal for any occasion. And, who doesn't have a box or two nestled on the shelf, just waiting to make that perfect meal? But a great pasta meal is more than just a box of pasta—it's the combination of pasta with other delicious ingredients in a way that makes you want to ask for more!

In *The Big Book of Pasta*, we provide that variety of pasta combinations and inspiring ideas for great meals any night of the week. Classic recipes include Fettuccine Alfredo, page 34, and Cacio e Pepe, page 32, among others. You'll also discover many new ideas, such as a wonderful Crab Scampi with Beer, page 110, or a new take on an old favorite, Bacon, Kale and Tomato Mac and Cheese, page 290. And why not try making pasta from scratch? It's easier than you think, and we provide recipes for a variety of shapes to choose from, including fettuccine, linguini and even filled ravioli. Look for whole wheat and gluten-free versions of homemade pasta too.

We know that getting dinner on the table quickly is always top of mind, so we've included features to help. Mix-and-Match Pasta and Sauce, page 88, helps with how to pair ingredients together. And if you need a great last-minute meal, there are features for that too. Jazz Up a Jar of Sauce, page 226, provides many ideas for you to try, and Three-Ingredient Pasta Sauces, page 168, is simply inspiration for quick meals.

So if you love pasta and are looking for new ideas, look no further—*The Big Book of Pasta* is all you need.

Enjoy!
Betty Crocker

Look for these helpful icons:
- **QUICK** • = 30 min. or less, total
- **MEATLESS** •

contents

Introduction

Whether mixed in a comforting casserole or simply tossed with a sensational sauce, the meal possibilities with dried, fresh or frozen or even homemade pasta are endless — but always enjoyable.

With a few handy tips, you'll have all that you need to make pasta that is tender, delicious and the star of the meal.

Purchasing Pointers

- **Dried Pasta:** Avoid broken pasta or pasta that looks cracked. It may fall apart during cooking. Be sure to check sell-by dates on packages because pasta past its prime may not perform well.

- **Fresh Pasta:** Avoid packages with moisture droplets or liquid inside. Pasta should be smooth and evenly colored without broken or crumbly pieces. Look for sell-by dates too.

- **Frozen Pasta:** Avoid packages that are frozen as a solid block and those with ice crystals or freezer burn (dry, white spots).

Storage Tips

- **Dried Pasta:** Label, date and store tightly covered in a cool, dry place up to 1 year.

- **Fresh Pasta:** Refrigerate and use by date on package. Store opened, uncooked pasta in a tightly covered container up to 3 days.

- **Frozen Pasta:** Freeze unopened fresh pasta in the original package up to 9 months. Leftover uncooked pasta can be frozen in a tightly covered container up to 3 months and homemade fresh pasta up to 1 month.

- **Cooked Pasta:** To prevent sticking during storage, toss cooked pasta with 1 to 2 teaspoons olive or vegetable oil after draining. Refrigerate tightly covered up to 5 days, or freeze up to 2 months.

Pasta Yields

Plan on ½ to ¾ cup cooked pasta per side dish and 1 to 1½ cups per main-dish serving.

To easily measure 4 ounces of dried spaghetti, make a circle with your thumb and index finger (about the size of a quarter) and fill it with pasta.

Type of Pasta	Uncooked	Cooked	Servings
Short Pastas Penne, Rotini, Shells, Wagon Wheels	6 to 7 oz	4 cups	4 to 6
Long Pastas Capellini, Linguine, Spaghetti, Vermicelli	7 to 8 oz	4 cups	4 to 6
Egg Noodles	8 oz	4 to 5 cups	4 to 6

Tips for Cooking Pasta

- Use 1 quart (4 cups) water for every 4 ounces of pasta. When the water is boiling vigorously, gradually add the pasta. Reduce the heat just a bit so that the pasta can boil gently, and stir frequently to prevent sticking.

- For added flavor, add ½ teaspoon salt for every 8 ounces of pasta. Add the salt just as the water comes to a boil.

- Follow package directions for the correct cook times. For baked recipes, slightly undercook the pasta because it will continue to cook during baking.

- Cooked pasta should be al dente, or tender but firm to the bite, without any raw flavor. Overcooked pasta is mushy, waterlogged and bland.

- Unless the recipe specifies, do not rinse pasta after draining or sauces will not cling well. Pasta is usually rinsed only for cold salads.

Spinach Fettuccine

Gnocchi

Mini Gnocchi

Cellophane Noodles

Cheese Ravioletti

Cheese Ravioli

Long Ziti

Vermicelli

Angel Hair

Orzo

Sausage Ravioli

Cheese Tortellini

Spinach Cheese Tortellini

Fusilli Bucati

Couscous (large)

Ditalini

Rigatoni

Ziti

Lasagnotte

Couscous

Lasagna

Acini de Pepe

Mafalde

Spaghetti

Brown Rice Gluten Free Spaghetti

Linguine

CHAPTER 1

Signature Pasta & Sauces

homemade pasta

prep time: 30 Minutes • **start to finish:** 1 Hour 15 Minutes • 8 servings

2   cups all-purpose flour
½   teaspoon salt
2   eggs
¼   cup water
1   tablespoon olive or
    vegetable oil

Improvise

Add 1 tablespoon chopped fresh or 1 teaspoon dried crumbled herb leaves to flour mixture before adding eggs.

For Whole Wheat Pasta, make as directed, except use 3 cups whole wheat or white whole wheat flour and 5 eggs, beaten. Omit water.

Pasta Point

Use a large wooden board or laminated countertop for rolling out pasta dough. Avoid cold surfaces like granite, metal or marble because the dough tends to stick.

1 In medium bowl, mix flour and salt. Make a well in center of flour mixture. Add eggs, water and oil to well; mix thoroughly. (If dough is too dry, mix in enough water to make dough easy to handle. If dough is too sticky, gradually add flour when kneading.)

2 Gather dough into a ball. On lightly floured surface, knead 5 to 10 minutes or until smooth and springy. Cover with plastic wrap or foil; let stand 15 minutes.

3 Divide dough into 4 equal parts. On lightly floured surface, roll one-fourth of dough at a time (keep remaining dough covered) into rectangle, 1/16 to 1/8 inch thick (if using a hand-crank pasta machine, pass dough through machine until 1/16 inch thick*). Loosely fold rectangle lengthwise into thirds. Cut crosswise into 2-inch strips for lasagna, ¼-inch strips for fettuccine or 1/8-inch strips for linguine. Unfold and gently shake out strips. Hang pasta on pasta drying rack, or arrange in single layer on lightly floured towels; let stand 30 minutes or until dry.

4 In 6- to 8-quart Dutch oven or saucepan, heat 4 quarts water (salted if desired) to boiling; add pasta. Boil uncovered 2 to 5 minutes, stirring occasionally, until firm but tender. Begin testing for doneness when pasta rises to surface of water; drain.

*Our recipes were not developed for or tested in electric extrusion pasta machines. These machines generally have specific measuring devices for dry and liquid ingredients unique to each machine. We recommend following the manufacturer's directions.

1 Serving: Calories 150; Total Fat 3.5g (Saturated Fat 0.5g; Trans Fat 0g); Cholesterol 55mg; Sodium 160mg; Total Carbohydrate 24g (Dietary Fiber 0g); Protein 5g **Exchanges:** 1½ Starch, ½ Fat **Carbohydrate Choices:** 1½

Cutting Homemade Pasta

On lightly floured surface, roll one-fourth of dough at a time into rectangle, $\frac{1}{16}$ to $\frac{1}{8}$ inch thick (keep remaining dough covered).

Loosely fold rectangle lengthwise into thirds.

Cut pasta crosswise into 2-inch strips for lasagna, $\frac{1}{4}$-inch strips for fettuccine or $\frac{1}{8}$-inch strips for linguine.

Unfold and gently shake out strips. Hang strips on pasta drying rack, or arrange in single layer on lightly floured towels.

gluten-free homemade pasta

prep time: 30 Minutes • **start to finish:** 1 Hour 15 Minutes • **8 servings**

2 cups Betty Crocker™ Gluten Free all-purpose rice flour blend

½ teaspoon salt

2 eggs

⅓ cup water

1 tablespoon olive or vegetable oil

1 In medium bowl, mix flour blend and salt. Make a well in center of mixture. Add eggs, water and oil to well; mix thoroughly. (If dough is too dry, mix in water, 1 teaspoon at a time, until dough is easy to handle. If dough is too sticky, gradually add flour blend when kneading.) Gather dough into a ball. On surface lightly sprinkled with flour blend, knead 3 to 5 minutes or until firm and smooth. Cover with plastic wrap or foil; let stand 15 minutes.

2 Divide dough into 6 equal parts.* On surface lightly sprinkled with flour blend, roll one-sixth of dough at a time (keep remaining dough covered or it will dry out and crack) into rectangle, ¹⁄₁₆ to ⅛ inch thick (if using hand-crank pasta machine, pass dough through machine until ¹⁄₁₆ inch thick**). Loosely fold rectangle lengthwise into thirds. Cut crosswise into 2-inch strips for lasagna, ¼-inch strips for fettuccine or ⅛-inch strips for linguine. Unfold and gently shake out strips. Hang pasta on pasta drying rack or arrange in single layer on towels lightly sprinkled with flour blend; let stand 30 minutes or until dry.

3 In 6- to 8-quart Dutch oven or saucepan, heat 4 quarts water (salted if desired) to boiling; add pasta. Boil uncovered 2 to 5 minutes, stirring occasionally, until firm but tender. Begin testing for doneness when pasta rises to surface of water; drain.

*Gluten-free pasta dough is more fragile and can break more easily. We found working with smaller dough portions and keeping dough sheets 12 inches or shorter worked best.

**Our recipes were not developed for or tested in electric extrusion pasta machines. These machines generally have specific measuring devices for dry and liquid ingredients unique to each machine. We recommend following the manufacturer's directions.

1 Serving: Calories 150; Total Fat 3.5g (Saturated Fat 0.5g; Trans Fat 0g); Cholesterol 55mg; Sodium 160mg; Total Carbohydrate 24g (Dietary Fiber 0g); Protein 5g
Exchanges: 1½ Starch, ½ Fat **Carbohydrate Choices:** 1½

marinara sauce

prep time: 15 Minutes • **start to finish:** 45 Minutes • 12 servings

2 cans (28 oz each) crushed tomatoes with basil, undrained

1 can (6 oz) tomato paste

1 large onion, chopped (1 cup)

8 cloves garlic, finely chopped

1 tablespoon olive or vegetable oil

2 teaspoons sugar

1½ teaspoons dried basil leaves

1 teaspoon dried oregano leaves

1 teaspoon pepper

½ teaspoon salt

1 In 3-quart saucepan, stir all ingredients until well mixed. Heat to boiling; reduce heat to low. Cover; simmer 30 minutes to blend flavors.

2 Use sauce immediately, or cover and refrigerate up to 2 weeks or freeze up to 1 year.

1 Serving: Calories 130; Total Fat 2g (Saturated Fat 0g; Trans Fat 0g); Cholesterol 0mg; Sodium 900mg; Total Carbohydrate 24g (Dietary Fiber 4g); Protein 4g **Exchanges:** ½ Starch, 1 Other Carbohydrate, ½ Vegetable, ½ Fat **Carbohydrate Choices:** 1½

puttanesca

prep time: 40 Minutes • start to finish: 40 Minutes • 4 servings

⅓ cup olive or vegetable oil

2 cloves garlic, halved

1 tablespoon capers

4 flat anchovy fillets in oil, drained, finely chopped

2 cans (28 oz each) whole tomatoes, drained, chopped

1 small jalapeño chile, seeded, finely chopped

1 package (16 oz) spaghetti

½ cup sliced pitted kalamata or ripe black olives

1 In 4-quart Dutch oven or saucepan, heat oil over medium-high heat. Cook garlic in oil, stirring frequently, until golden. Remove garlic and discard.

2 Stir capers, anchovy fillets, tomatoes and chile into oil in Dutch oven. Heat to boiling; reduce heat. Simmer uncovered 15 minutes.

3 Meanwhile, cook and drain spaghetti as directed on package. Stir spaghetti and olives into tomato mixture; cook until thoroughly heated.

1 Serving: Calories 750; Total Fat 24g (Saturated Fat 3.5g; Trans Fat 0g); Cholesterol 0mg; Sodium 790mg; Total Carbohydrate 112g (Dietary Fiber 9g); Protein 22g
Exchanges: 6 Starch, ½ Other Carbohydrate, 2½ Vegetable, 4 Fat
Carbohydrate Choices: 7½

bolognese

prep time: 25 Minutes • start to finish: 1 Hour 10 Minutes • 12 servings

2 tablespoons olive or vegetable oil

1 tablespoon butter

2 medium carrots, finely chopped (1 cup)

1 medium stalk celery, finely chopped (½ cup)

1 medium onion, chopped (½ cup)

2 cloves garlic, finely chopped

1 lb lean (at least 80%) ground beef

¼ cup chopped pancetta or bacon

½ cup dry red wine, nonalcoholic red wine or beef broth

3 cans (28 oz each) whole tomatoes, drained, chopped

1 teaspoon dried oregano leaves

½ teaspoon pepper

½ cup milk or heavy whipping cream

1 In 12-inch skillet, heat oil and butter over medium-high heat. Add carrots, celery, onion and garlic; cook, stirring frequently, until crisp-tender. Stir in beef and pancetta. Cook 8 to 10 minutes, stirring occasionally, until beef is thoroughly cooked; drain.

2 Stir in wine. Heat to boiling; reduce heat to low. Simmer uncovered until wine has evaporated. Stir in tomatoes, oregano and pepper. Heat to boiling; reduce heat to low. Cover and simmer 45 minutes, stirring occasionally. Remove from heat; stir in milk.

3 Use sauce immediately, or cover and refrigerate up to 48 hours or freeze up to 2 months.

1 Serving: Calories 100; Total Fat 4g (Saturated Fat 1g; Trans Fat 0g); Cholesterol 25mg; Sodium 360mg; Total Carbohydrate 8g (Dietary Fiber 2g); Protein 9g **Exchanges:** 1½ Vegetable, 1 Medium-Fat Meat **Carbohydrate Choices:** ½

....

Pasta Point

A staple of Northern Italy, bolognese is a hearty, thick meat sauce with canned tomatoes, wine and milk or cream. Think of it as a meat sauce with tomato versus a tomato sauce with meat.

creamy tomato-vodka sauce

prep time: 10 Minutes • **start to finish:** 30 Minutes • 6 servings

1 tablespoon olive or
  vegetable oil

1 small onion, chopped
  (⅓ cup)

2 cloves garlic,
  finely chopped

1 can (28 oz) crushed
  tomatoes with basil,
  undrained

½ cup vodka or chicken broth

1 teaspoon sugar

¼ teaspoon coarse
  (kosher or sea) salt

⅛ teaspoon pepper

½ cup heavy whipping cream

1 In 10-inch skillet, heat oil over medium heat. Cook onion and garlic in oil 3 to 4 minutes, stirring constantly, until crisp-tender.

2 Stir in tomatoes, vodka, sugar, salt and pepper. Heat to boiling. Reduce heat; simmer 20 minutes, stirring occasionally. Stir in whipping cream. Heat just until hot.

1 Serving: Calories 130; Total Fat 9g (Saturated Fat 4g; Trans Fat 0g); Cholesterol 20mg; Sodium 270mg; Total Carbohydrate 8g (Dietary Fiber 1g); Protein 2g **Exchanges:** 1 Vegetable, 2 Fat **Carbohydrate Choices:** ½

italian tomato sauce

prep time: 15 Minutes • start to finish: 1 Hour 5 Minutes • 8 servings

- 2 tablespoons olive or vegetable oil
- 1 large onion, chopped (1 cup)
- 1 small green bell pepper, chopped (½ cup)
- 2 large cloves garlic, finely chopped
- 1 can (28 oz) whole tomatoes, undrained
- 2 cans (8 oz each) tomato sauce
- 2 tablespoons chopped fresh or 2 teaspoons dried basil leaves
- 1 tablespoon chopped fresh or 1 teaspoon dried oregano leaves
- ½ teaspoon salt
- ½ teaspoon fennel seed
- ¼ teaspoon pepper

1 In 3-quart saucepan, heat oil over medium heat. Cook onion, bell pepper and garlic in oil 2 minutes, stirring occasionally.

2 Stir in remaining ingredients, breaking up tomatoes with fork. Heat to boiling; reduce heat. Simmer uncovered 45 minutes, stirring occasionally.

3 Use sauce immediately, or cover and refrigerate up to 2 weeks or freeze up to 1 year.

1 Serving: Calories 90; Total Fat 3.5g (Saturated Fat 0g; Trans Fat 0g); Cholesterol 0mg; Sodium 670mg; Total Carbohydrate 11g (Dietary Fiber 2g); Protein 2g **Exchanges:** 2 Vegetable, ½ Fat **Carbohydrate Choices:** 1

• •

Improvise

To make in the slow cooker, use 1 medium onion, chopped (½ cup). Substitute 1 can (28 ounces) diced tomatoes, undrained, for the whole tomatoes. Use 1 can (8 ounces) tomato sauce. Spray 3½ to 6-quart slow cooker with cooking spray. In slow cooker, mix all ingredients. Cover; cook on Low heat setting 8 to 10 hours.

• •

Pasta Point

Make a batch or two and freeze it in portion sizes that work for you. Use it as is, or toss in some pepperoni, cooked Italian sausage and mushrooms or olives.

arrabbiata pasta sauce

prep time: 10 Minutes • **start to finish:** 25 Minutes • 4 servings

1 tablespoon olive or vegetable oil

3 cloves garlic, finely chopped

1 can (28 oz) crushed tomatoes with basil, undrained

½ teaspoon crushed red pepper flakes

½ teaspoon coarse (kosher or sea) salt

⅛ teaspoon pepper

1 In 3-quart saucepan, heat oil over medium heat. Cook garlic in oil about 1 minute, stirring constantly, until golden.

2 Stir in remaining ingredients. Heat to boiling. Reduce heat; simmer uncovered about 15 minutes, stirring occasionally, until thickened.

3 Serve over cooked pasta.

1 Serving: Calories 70; Total Fat 3.5g (Saturated Fat 0.5g; Trans Fat 0g); Cholesterol 0mg; Sodium 550mg; Total Carbohydrate 9g (Dietary Fiber 2g); Protein 2g **Exchanges:** 1 Vegetable, 1 Fat **Carbohydrate Choices:** ½

Pasta Points

Be sure to cook the garlic just until golden. If the garlic burns, the sauce will have a bitter, unpleasant flavor.

Ah-rah-bee-AH-tah is the Italian word for "angry" and refers to culinary dishes with lots of spice. Tomatoes, pancetta and chiles are often used. The crushed red pepper flakes and garlic give its signature spice.

short rib–sausage ragu

prep time: 35 Minutes • **start to finish:** 3 Hours 35 Minutes • **8 servings**

- 3 lb boneless beef short ribs
- 1 teaspoon salt
- 2 tablespoons olive oil
- ¼ cup finely chopped carrot
- ¼ cup finely chopped celery
- ¼ cup finely chopped onion
- 2 cloves garlic, finely chopped
- 4 oz mild bulk Italian pork sausage
- ½ cup dry red wine
- 2 tablespoons tomato paste
- 1 tablespoon all-purpose flour
- 2½ cups reduced-sodium beef broth
- ¼ teaspoon pepper
- 2 slices bacon, crisply cooked, crumbled
- 2 sprigs fresh thyme (about 5 inches long)
- 2 sprigs fresh rosemary (about 5 inches long)
- Hot cooked pappardelle or rigatoni pasta, if desired
- Shredded Parmesan cheese, if desired

1 Heat oven to 350°F. Sprinkle ribs with salt and rub it into all surfaces. In 6-quart Dutch oven or saucepan, heat oil over medium-high heat. Cook ribs in oil 6 to 8 minutes, turning frequently, until browned on all sides (brown ribs in batches if necessary). Remove ribs; set aside.

2 Reduce heat to medium. Add carrots, celery, onion, garlic and sausage to Dutch oven. Cook 6 to 8 minutes, stirring frequently and scraping up any browned bits, until sausage is browned. Drain any fat if necessary. Stir in wine; heat to boiling. Reduce heat; simmer uncovered about 6 minutes or until wine is almost evaporated.

3 Stir in tomato paste and flour until well blended. Gradually stir in 2½ cups of the broth; stir in pepper and bacon. Place herb sprigs on counter and tie together with kitchen string, place in broth. Place ribs into broth, coating with broth on all sides. Ribs may not fit in a single layer and will not be submerged in broth mixture.

4 Cover and bake 2½ to 3 hours or until ribs are starting to fall apart when tested with fork and are well browned. Remove ribs. Skim off fat from sausage, bacon and any sauce mixture in Dutch oven and discard. Cut excess fat from ribs and discard. Pull ribs into 1-inch pieces; return to reserved sausage and bacon mixture in Dutch oven and toss to coat. Heat until hot. Serve over pasta; sprinkle with cheese.

1 Serving: Calories 440; Total Fat 31g (Saturated Fat 11g; Trans Fat 1g); Cholesterol 125mg; Sodium 750mg; Total Carbohydrate 3g (Dietary Fiber 0g, Sugars 1g); Protein 35g **Exchanges:** 5 Medium-Fat Meat, 1 Fat **Carbohydrate Choices:** 0

basil pesto

prep time: 10 Minutes • **start to finish:** 10 Minutes • 10 servings

2 cups firmly packed fresh
  basil leaves

¾ cup grated
  Parmesan cheese

¼ cup pine nuts, toasted*
  if desired

½ cup olive or vegetable oil

3 cloves garlic

1 In blender or food processor, place all ingredients. Cover; blend on medium speed about 3 minutes, stopping occasionally to scrape down the sides with a rubber spatula, until smooth.

2 Use pesto immediately, or cover tightly and refrigerate up to 5 days or freeze up to 1 month (color of pesto will darken as it stands).

*To toast pine nuts, sprinkle in ungreased skillet. Cook over medium heat 5 to 7 minutes, stirring frequently until nuts begin to brown, then stirring constantly until nuts are light brown.

1 Serving: Calories 160; Total Fat 15g (Saturated Fat 3g; Trans Fat 0g); Cholesterol 5mg; Sodium 140mg; Total Carbohydrate 1g (Dietary Fiber 0g); Protein 4g **Exchanges:** ½ Vegetable, 3 Fat **Carbohydrate Choices:** 0

Improvise

For **bell pepper–basil pesto** use a food processor. Decrease basil to 1 cup. Decrease oil to ⅓ cup; add ½ cup drained roasted red or yellow bell peppers (from jar). Substitute walnuts for the pine nuts.

For **cilantro pesto**, substitute 1½ cups firmly packed fresh cilantro and ½ cup firmly packed fresh parsley for the basil.

For **spinach pesto**, substitute 2 cups firmly packed fresh spinach leaves for the basil.

For **sun-dried tomato pesto**, use a food processor. Omit basil. Decrease oil to ⅓ cup; add ½ cup sun-dried tomatoes in oil, undrained.

four-cheese homemade ravioli

prep time: 1 Hour • **start to finish:** 1 Hour 15 Minutes • 5 servings

PASTA

Homemade Pasta (page 12)

FILLING

¾ **cup ricotta cheese (from 15-oz container)**

¼ **cup shredded fontina cheese**

¼ **cup shredded Parmesan cheese**

¼ **cup shredded mozzarella cheese**

1 Make pasta as directed through step 2. Divide dough into 4 equal parts. On lightly floured surface, roll one-fourth of dough at a time (keep remaining dough covered with damp towel) into rectangle 1⁄16 to 1⁄8 inch thick (if using hand-crank pasta machine, pass dough through machine until 1⁄16 inch thick*). Cut dough into 4 (14x4-inch) rectangles. Cover with damp towel until ready to fill.

2 In medium bowl, mix filling ingredients until well blended. On 1 dough rectangle, place 5 mounds of filling (using slightly less than 1 measuring tablespoon for each mound) about 1½ inches apart in 2 rows. Moisten dough lightly around mounds with water; top with second rectangle of dough, lining up edges of sheets. Press gently around edges to seal. Cut between mounds, using pizza cutter or knife, into 10 squares. Trim any uneven edges and reseal if needed. Repeat with remaining dough and filling.

3 In 8-quart Dutch oven or stockpot, heat 4 quarts water (salted if desired) to boiling; add ravioli. Boil uncovered 7 to 10 minutes, stirring occasionally, until tender (ravioli will rise to the top during first few minutes). Remove ravioli with large slotted spoon to colander to drain; do not rinse. Do not dump pasta and water into colander to drain or ravioli will break open. Serve with your favorite sauce.

*Our recipes were not developed for or tested in electric extrusion pasta machines. These machines generally have specific measuring devices for dry and liquid ingredients unique to each machine. We recommend following the manufacturer's directions.

1 Serving (4 Ravioli): Calories 340; Total Fat 13g (Saturated Fat 6g, Trans Fat 0g); Cholesterol 100mg; Sodium 480mg; Total Carbohydrate 41g (Dietary Fiber 1g, Sugars 0g); Protein 16g **Exchanges:** 2 Starch, ½ Other Carbohydrate, 1½ Medium-Fat Meat, 1 Fat **Carbohydrate Choices:** 3

Ravioli Tips

Ravioli are fun to make and fun to eat. Because these are fairly large, allow 3 or 4 ravioli per serving. You can choose to eat them just tossed with olive oil and fresh herbs or with fresh pesto, or top them with a favorite tomato sauce.

Because ravioli are tender, gently stir while they are boiling. Then, lift the ravioli from the boiling water with a slotted spoon to keep these delicious morsels from breaking into pieces.

If you need to reheat ravioli, just plunge into boiling water for a couple of minutes and drain.

Bacon, Chive and Parmesan Ravioli

Four-Cheese Ravioli

Spicy Sausage, Sun-Dried Tomato and Mozzarella Ravioli

Bacon, Chive and Parmesan Ravioli

Make pasta as directed. Omit filling ingredients. In medium bowl, mix 1 container (8 ounces) chives-and-onion cream cheese, 6 slices bacon, crisply cooked and crumbled, and ¼ cup grated Parmesan cheese until well blended. Continue as directed.

Spicy Sausage, Sun-Dried Tomato and Mozzarella Ravioli

Make pasta as directed. Omit filling ingredients. In 8-inch skillet, cook ½ pound bulk spicy Italian pork sausage over medium heat, stirring occasionally, until no longer pink; drain. Place in medium bowl; cool 15 minutes. Add ¼ cup sun-dried tomatoes in oil, drained and chopped, ½ cup shredded mozzarella cheese (4 ounces) and 1 egg, beaten; mix well. Continue as directed.

Bacon,
Chive and
Parmesan
Ravioli

Four-Cheese
Ravioli

cacio e pepe

prep time: 25 Minutes • **start to finish:** 25 Minutes • 6 servings

1 package (16 oz) spaghetti

¼ cup olive oil

2 teaspoons coarse ground black pepper

1½ cups finely shredded Pecorino Romano cheese

Chopped fresh parsley, if desired

1 Cook pasta as directed on package, except remove 1 cup of pasta cooking water before draining pasta. Set aside the reserved pasta cooking water. Drain the pasta but do not rinse.

2 In 4-quart saucepan, heat oil over medium heat. Add pepper; cook and stir 1 minute to toast pepper. Add ¾ cup of the reserved pasta water and heat until simmering. Add pasta; sprinkle pasta with cheese. Toss with tongs to combine until mixture clings to pasta. If mixture seems dry, add remaining ¼ cup reserved pasta cooking water, but this pasta dish will not be saucy.

3 Sprinkle with parsley. Serve with additional cheese if desired.

1 Serving: Calories 520; Total Fat 19g (Saturated Fat 6g, Trans Fat 0g); Cholesterol 30mg; Sodium 640mg; Total Carbohydrate 67g (Dietary Fiber 4g, Sugars 1g); Protein 21g **Exchanges:** 4 Starch, ½ Other Carbohydrate, 1 High-Fat Meat, 2 Fat **Carbohydrate Choices:** 4½

• •

Pasta Point

Cacio e Pepe translates to "cheese and pepper" and is a very simple, zesty pasta dish that can be made quickly. There is no typo—the recipe really does have 2 teaspoons of pepper.

fettuccine alfredo

prep time: 25 Minutes • **start to finish:** 25 Minutes • 4 servings

8   oz uncooked fettuccine

½   cup butter, cut into pieces

½   cup heavy whipping cream

¾   cup grated
    Parmesan cheese

½   teaspoon salt

    Dash pepper

    Chopped fresh parsley,
    if desired

1 Cook and drain fettuccine as directed on package.

2 Meanwhile, in 10-inch skillet, heat butter and whipping cream over medium heat, stirring frequently, until butter is melted and mixture starts to bubble. Reduce heat to low; simmer uncovered 6 minutes, stirring frequently, until slightly thickened. Remove from heat. Stir in cheese, salt and pepper.

3 In large bowl, toss fettuccine with sauce until well coated. Sprinkle with parsley.

1 Serving: Calories 570; Total Fat 40g (Saturated Fat 21g; Trans Fat 2g); Cholesterol 155mg; Sodium 810mg; Total Carbohydrate 38g (Dietary Fiber 2g); Protein 15g
Exchanges: 2½ Starch, 1 High-Fat Meat, 5½ Fat **Carbohydrate Choices:** 2½

. . . .

Improvise

If you like, stir in 1½ cups diced cooked chicken with the cheese, salt and pepper.

. . . .

Pasta Point

To decrease the amount of fat to about 17 grams and calories to 370 per serving, reduce the butter to ¼ cup and the Parmesan cheese to ½ cup; substitute evaporated milk for the whipping cream.

macaroni and cheese

prep time: 25 Minutes • start to finish: 50 Minutes • 4 servings

1 package (7 oz) elbow macaroni (2½ cups)

¼ cup butter

¼ cup all-purpose flour

½ teaspoon salt

¼ teaspoon pepper

¼ teaspoon dry mustard

¼ teaspoon Worcestershire sauce

2 cups milk or half-and-half

2 cups shredded sharp Cheddar cheese

1 Heat oven to 350°F. Cook and drain macaroni as directed on package, using minimum cook time.

2 Meanwhile, in 3-quart saucepan, melt butter over low heat. Stir in flour, salt, pepper, mustard and Worcestershire sauce. Cook over low heat, stirring constantly, until mixture is smooth and bubbly; remove from heat.

3 Stir in milk. Heat to boiling, stirring constantly. Boil and stir 1 minute; remove from heat. Stir in cheese until melted. Gently stir macaroni into cheese sauce.

4 Pour into ungreased 2-quart casserole. Bake uncovered 20 to 25 minutes or until bubbly.

1 Serving : Calories 610; Total Fat 34g (Saturated Fat 19g; Trans Fat 1g); Cholesterol 100mg; Sodium 980mg; Total Carbohydrate 51g (Dietary Fiber 3g); Protein 26g
Exchanges: 3 Starch, ½ Low-Fat Milk, 2 High-Fat Meat, 2½ Fat
Carbohydrate Choices: 3½

Pasta Points

If you would prefer making this a stove-top recipe, cook and drain macaroni as directed on package. Continue as directed in steps 2 and 3; omit step 4.

For 10 grams of fat and 390 calories per serving, reduce butter to 2 tablespoons. Use fat-free (skim) milk and 1½ cups reduced-fat Cheddar cheese (6 ounces).

Improvise

Stir in ⅔ cup crumbled crisply cooked bacon with the macaroni in step 3.

Stir in ½ teaspoon smoked paprika with the flour in step 2. Add 1 can (14.5 ounces) fire-roasted diced tomatoes, drained, with the macaroni in step 3.

Add ⅛ teaspoon each ground red pepper (cayenne) and ground nutmeg with the flour in step 2. Substitute ¾ cup each shredded fontina and Gruyère cheese for 1½ cups of the Cheddar. Stir in 2 cups cooked lobster pieces with the macaroni in step 3.

Omit ground mustard and Worcestershire sauce. Add 2 teaspoons ground ancho chile pepper or chili powder, ½ teaspoon ground cumin and ¼ teaspoon garlic powder with the flour in step 2. Stir in 1 can (4.5 ounces) diced green chiles, ¼ cup thinly sliced green onions, ¼ cup diced bell pepper and ¼ cup chopped fresh cilantro with the macaroni in step 3. Top with coarsely crushed corn chips before serving.

creamy noodles romanoff

prep time: 10 Minutes • start to finish: 25 Minutes • 4 servings

4   cups uncooked wide egg
    noodles (8 oz)

2   cups sour cream

¼   cup grated
    Parmesan cheese

1   tablespoon chopped
    fresh chives

½   teaspoon salt

⅛   teaspoon pepper

2   cloves garlic,
    finely chopped

2   tablespoons butter

1 Cook and drain noodles as directed on package. In small bowl, stir together sour cream, 2 tablespoons of the cheese, chives, salt, pepper and garlic.

2 Stir butter into noodles. Stir in sour cream mixture. Sprinkle with remaining 2 tablespoons cheese.

1 Serving: Calories 460; Total Fat 33g (Saturated Fat 19g; Trans Fat 1g); Cholesterol 110mg; Sodium 730mg; Total Carbohydrate 32g (Dietary Fiber 1g); Protein 10g
Exchanges: 2 Starch, ½ Lean Meat, 6 Fat **Carbohydrate Choices:** 2

. . . .

Pasta Point

You can decrease fat and calories, but not taste, by using reduced-fat sour cream and reduced-fat Parmesan cheese blend and by decreasing the margarine to 1 tablespoon.

. . . .

Pasta Pairing

Pair the noodles with mixed salad greens and honey whole wheat rolls for a simple meal. This pasta can be served as a main dish but would also be a perfect side dish served with grilled chicken or steak.

primavera pasta

prep time: 25 Minutes • **start to finish:** 25 Minutes • **4 servings (1½ cups each)**

8 oz uncooked fettuccine

1 tablespoon olive or vegetable oil

1 cup fresh broccoli florets

1 cup fresh cauliflower florets

1 cup frozen sweet peas

2 medium carrots, thinly sliced (1 cup)

1 small onion, chopped (⅓ cup)

1 container (10 oz) refrigerated Alfredo pasta sauce

¼ cup milk

1 tablespoon Dijon mustard

1 oz shaved Parmesan cheese

1 Cook and drain fettuccine as directed on package.

2 Meanwhile, in 12-inch skillet, heat oil over medium-high heat. Add broccoli, cauliflower, peas, carrots and onion; cook 6 to 8 minutes, stirring frequently, until vegetables are crisp-tender.

3 Stir Alfredo sauce, milk and mustard into vegetable mixture; cook until hot. Stir in fettuccine; cook until thoroughly heated. Top with cheese.

1 Serving: Calories 570; Total Fat 31g (Saturated Fat 16g; Trans Fat 1g); Cholesterol 120mg; Sodium 580mg; Total Carbohydrate 55g (Dietary Fiber 5g); Protein 18g **Exchanges:** 3 Starch, 2 Vegetable, ½ High-Fat Meat, 5 Fat **Carbohydrate Choices:** 3½

. . . .

Improvise

Look for refrigerated Alfredo sauce next to the fresh pasta in your grocery store refrigerator case. If you're counting calories and fat, purchase "light" Alfredo sauce.

Try substituting linguine or spaghetti for the fettuccine.

manicotti

prep time: 40 Minutes • **start to finish:** 1 Hour 35 Minutes • 7 servings

14 uncooked manicotti
    pasta shells

1   lb lean (at least 80%)
    ground beef

1   cup sliced fresh mushrooms
    (3 oz) or 1 can (4 oz)
    mushroom pieces and
    stems, drained

1   large onion, chopped
    (1 cup)

2   cloves garlic,
    finely chopped

1   jar (24 to 28 oz) tomato
    pasta sauce

2   boxes (9 oz each) frozen
    chopped spinach, thawed

2   cups small-curd
    cottage cheese

⅓   cup grated
    Parmesan cheese

¼   teaspoon ground nutmeg

¼   teaspoon pepper

2   cups shredded
    mozzarella cheese

2   tablespoons grated
    Parmesan cheese

1 Cook and drain pasta shells as directed on package, using minimum cook time. Meanwhile, in 10-inch skillet, cook beef, mushrooms, onion and garlic over medium heat 8 to 10 minutes, stirring occasionally, until beef is thoroughly cooked; drain. Stir in pasta sauce. Heat oven to 350°F. Spray 13x9-inch (3-quart) glass baking dish with cooking spray.

2 Squeeze thawed spinach to drain; spread on paper towels and pat dry. In medium bowl, mix spinach, cottage cheese, ⅓ cup Parmesan cheese, the nutmeg and pepper.

3 In baking dish, spread 1 cup of the beef mixture. Fill pasta shells with spinach mixture; place on beef mixture in dish. Pour remaining beef mixture evenly over shells, covering completely. Sprinkle with mozzarella cheese and 2 tablespoons Parmesan cheese.

4 Cover and bake 30 minutes. Uncover; bake 20 to 25 minutes longer or until hot and bubbly.

1 Serving: Calories 570; Total Fat 21g (Saturated Fat 10g; Trans Fat 0.5g); Cholesterol 70mg; Sodium 1360mg; Total Carbohydrate 55g (Dietary Fiber 6g); Protein 39g
Exchanges: 2½ Starch, 1 Other Carbohydrate, 4½ Lean Meat, 1 Fat
Carbohydrate Choices: 3½

spaghetti and meatballs

prep time: 1 Hour 45 minutes • start to finish: 2 Hours 10 Minutes • 6 servings

Italian Tomato Sauce
(page 20)

1 lb lean (at least 80%)
ground beef

½ cup unseasoned dry
bread crumbs

¼ cup milk

½ teaspoon salt

½ teaspoon
Worcestershire sauce

¼ teaspoon pepper

1 small onion, finely chopped
(⅓ cup)

1 egg

4 cups hot cooked spaghetti

Grated or shredded
Parmesan cheese, if desired

1 Make tomato sauce.

2 Heat oven to 400°F. In large bowl, mix ground beef, bread crumbs, milk, salt, Worcestershire sauce, pepper, onion and egg. Shape mixture into 24 (1¼-inch) meatballs. Place in ungreased 13x9-inch pan or on rack in broiler pan. Bake uncovered 20 to 25 minutes or until no longer pink in center and thermometer inserted in center reads 160°F.

3 Stir meatballs into sauce. Simmer uncovered over low heat 30 minutes, stirring occasionally. Serve over spaghetti. Sprinkle with cheese.

1 Serving: Calories 430; Total Fat 16g (Saturated Fat 4.5g; Trans Fat 0.5g); Cholesterol 85mg; Sodium 1320mg; Total Carbohydrate 49g (Dietary Fiber 6g); Protein 23g
Exchanges: 2 Starch, ½ Other Carbohydrate, 2 Vegetable, 2 Medium-Fat Meat, 1 Fat
Carbohydrate Choices: 3

Improvise

For Spaghetti with Meat Sauce, omit the meatballs. In 10-inch skillet, cook 1 pound lean (at least 80%) ground beef or bulk Italian pork sausage, 1 large onion, chopped (1 cup), and 2 cloves garlic, finely chopped, over medium heat 8 to 10 minutes, stirring occasionally, until meat is thoroughly cooked; drain. Stir meat mixture into sauce. Simmer as directed in step 3.

You can use ground turkey or chicken in place of the ground beef for the meatballs. If using ground chicken, decrease milk to 2 tablespoons.

If you prefer to make the meatballs in a skillet, heat 10-inch skillet. Cook meatballs over medium heat about 20 minutes, turning occasionally, until no longer pink in center and thermometer inserted in center reads 160°F.

beef with bow tie pasta

prep time: 20 Minutes • **start to finish:** 20 Minutes • 6 servings

1½ lb boneless beef
    sirloin steak

3 cups 2-inch pieces
   asparagus (1 lb)

2 medium onions, sliced

1½ cups beef broth
    (from 32-oz carton)

4 cups cooked bow-tie
   (farfalle) pasta

1 cup tomato puree
   (from 28-oz can)

3 tablespoons chopped
   fresh or 1 tablespoon dried
   basil leaves

3 tablespoons chopped
   sun-dried tomatoes
   (not oil-packed)

¼ teaspoon pepper

2 tablespoons shredded
   Parmesan cheese

1 Trim fat from beef. Cut beef with grain into 2-inch strips; cut strips across grain into ⅛-inch slices. (For easier cutting, partially freeze beef about 1 hour.)

2 Spray 12-inch skillet with cooking spray; heat over medium heat. Add asparagus, onions and 1 cup of the broth. Cook 5 to 7 minutes, stirring occasionally, until liquid has evaporated; remove mixture from skillet.

3 Add beef to skillet; cook about 2 minutes over medium heat, stirring frequently, until beef is no longer pink.

4 Return asparagus mixture to skillet. Stir in pasta, remaining broth and remaining ingredients except cheese. Cook about 2 minutes, stirring frequently, until mixture is hot. Sprinkle with cheese.

1 Serving: Calories 360; Total Fat 6g (Saturated Fat 2g; Trans Fat 0g); Cholesterol 75mg; Sodium 670mg; Total Carbohydrate 39g (Dietary Fiber 4g); Protein 38g **Exchanges:** 1½ Starch, ½ Other Carbohydrate, 2 Vegetable, 3 Very Lean Meat, 1 Lean Meat **Carbohydrate Choices:** 2½

• •

Improvise

Substitute crumbled feta cheese for the Parmesan cheese, and stir in ¼ cup capers.

skillet lasagna

prep time: 30 Minutes • **start to finish:** 30 Minutes • **4 servings**

1 lb lean (at least 80%) ground beef

1 small onion, chopped (⅓ cup)

1 small green bell pepper, chopped (½ cup)

1½ cups uncooked mini-lasagna (mafalda) noodles (3 oz)

1¼ cups water

¼ teaspoon Italian seasoning

1 jar (14 oz) tomato pasta sauce (any variety) or marinara sauce

1 jar (4.5 oz) sliced mushrooms, drained

⅓ cup shredded mozzarella cheese, if desired

1 In 12-inch skillet, cook beef, onion and bell pepper over medium-high heat about 6 minutes, stirring occasionally, until beef is browned; drain.

2 Stir in remaining ingredients except cheese. Heat to boiling, stirring occasionally; reduce heat to low. Simmer uncovered 10 to 12 minutes or until pasta is tender, stirring occasionally. Sprinkle with cheese.

1 Serving: Calories 370; Total Fat 15g (Saturated Fat 5g; Trans Fat 1g); Cholesterol 70mg; Sodium 630mg; Total Carbohydrate 32g (Dietary Fiber 3g); Protein 25g **Exchanges:** 2 Starch, 1 Vegetable, 2½ Lean Meat, 1½ Fat **Carbohydrate Choices:** 2

Improvise

Break up lasagna noodles or use pieces that are already broken instead of the mafalda pasta in this savory weeknight favorite.

If you're out of mozzarella but still want a cheesy experience, you can use shredded Parmesan, Asiago or Monterey Jack cheese instead.

italian sausage lasagna

prep time: 1 Hour • **start to finish:** 2 Hours • **8 servings**

1 lb bulk Italian pork sausage or lean (at least 80%) ground beef

1 medium onion, chopped (½ cup)

1 clove garlic, finely chopped

3 tablespoons chopped fresh parsley

1 tablespoon chopped fresh or 1 teaspoon dried basil leaves

1 teaspoon sugar

1 can (15 oz) tomato sauce

1 can (14.5 oz) whole tomatoes, undrained

8 uncooked lasagna noodles

1 container (15 to 16 oz) ricotta cheese or small-curd cottage cheese

½ cup grated Parmesan cheese

1 tablespoon chopped fresh or 1½ teaspoons dried oregano leaves

2 cups shredded mozzarella cheese

1 In 10-inch skillet, cook meat, onion and garlic over medium heat 8 to 10 minutes, stirring occasionally, until meat is no longer pink; drain.

2 Stir in 2 tablespoons of the parsley, the basil, sugar, tomato sauce and tomatoes, breaking up tomatoes. Heat to boiling, stirring occasionally; reduce heat. Simmer uncovered about 45 minutes or until slightly thickened.

3 Heat oven to 350°F. Cook and drain noodles as directed on package, using minimum cook time. Meanwhile, in small bowl, mix ricotta cheese, ¼ cup of the Parmesan cheese, the oregano and remaining 1 tablespoon parsley.

4 In ungreased 13x9-inch (3-quart) glass baking dish, spread half of the meat mixture (about 2 cups). Top with 4 noodles. Spread half of the cheese mixture (about 1 cup) over noodles. Sprinkle with half of the mozzarella cheese. Repeat layers, ending with mozzarella. Sprinkle with remaining ¼ cup Parmesan cheese.

5 Cover and bake 30 minutes. Uncover; bake about 15 minutes longer or until hot and bubbly. Let stand 15 minutes before cutting.

1 Serving: Calories 430; Total Fat 23g (Saturated Fat 11g; Trans Fat 0g); Cholesterol 70mg; Sodium 1110mg; Total Carbohydrate 28g (Dietary Fiber 3g); Protein 28g **Exchanges:** 2 Starch, 3 Medium-Fat Meat, 1 Fat **Carbohydrate Choices:** 2

Pasta Point

Cover unbaked lasagna with foil; refrigerate up to 24 hours or freeze up to 2 months. Bake covered 45 minutes, then bake uncovered 15 to 20 minutes longer (35 to 45 minutes if frozen) until hot and bubbly.

Improvise

For a meat-free lasagna, substitute 4 cups (from two 26- to 28-ounce jars) tomato pasta sauce with meat for the first 8 ingredients. Omit steps 1 and 2.

chicken tetrazzini

prep time: 20 Minutes • **start to finish:** 50 Minutes • 6 servings

7 oz uncooked spaghetti, broken into thirds

¼ cup butter

¼ cup all-purpose flour

½ teaspoon salt

¼ teaspoon pepper

1 cup chicken broth

1 cup heavy whipping cream

2 tablespoons dry sherry or water

2 cups cubed cooked chicken or turkey

1 jar (4.5 oz) sliced mushrooms, drained

½ cup grated Parmesan cheese

1 Heat oven to 350°F. Cook and drain spaghetti as directed on package, using minimum cook time.

2 Meanwhile, in 2-quart saucepan, melt butter over low heat. Stir in flour, salt and pepper. Cook and stir until mixture is smooth and bubbly; remove from heat. Stir in broth and whipping cream. Heat to boiling, stirring constantly. Boil and stir 1 minute.

3 Stir spaghetti, sherry, chicken and mushrooms into sauce. Spoon into ungreased 2-quart casserole. Sprinkle with cheese. Bake uncovered about 30 minutes or until bubbly in center.

1 Serving: Calories 470; Total Fat 27g (Saturated Fat 14g; Trans Fat 1g); Cholesterol 110mg; Sodium 810mg; Total Carbohydrate 33g (Dietary Fiber 2g); Protein 23g **Exchanges:** 2 Starch, 2½ Medium-Fat Meat, 2½ Fat **Carbohydrate Choices:** 2

straw and hay pasta

prep time: 40 Minutes • start to finish: 40 Minutes • 4 servings

1 tablespoon butter

1½ cups sliced fresh
mushrooms (4 oz)

4 oz fully cooked ham, cut
into 1x¼-inch strips

2 tablespoons chopped
fresh parsley

2 tablespoons chopped onion

¼ cup brandy or
chicken broth

1 cup heavy whipping cream

¼ teaspoon salt

¼ teaspoon pepper

1 package (9 oz)
refrigerated fettuccine

1 package (9 oz) refrigerated
spinach fettuccine

½ cup shredded
Parmesan cheese

Freshly ground pepper

1 In 10-inch skillet, melt butter over medium-high heat. Cook mushrooms, ham, parsley and onion in butter, stirring occasionally, until mushrooms are tender. Stir in brandy. Cook uncovered until liquid has evaporated.

2 Stir in whipping cream, salt and pepper. Heat to boiling; reduce heat. Simmer uncovered about 15 minutes, stirring frequently, until thickened.

3 Cook and drain fettuccine as directed on packages. In large bowl, toss fettuccine and sauce. Sprinkle with cheese and freshly ground pepper.

1 Serving: Calories 760; Total Fat 33g (Saturated Fat 17g; Trans Fat 1g); Cholesterol 210mg; Sodium 860mg; Total Carbohydrate 87g (Dietary Fiber 4g); Protein 30g
Exchanges: 5 Starch, 2 Vegetable, ½ High-Fat Meat, 3 Fat **Carbohydrate Choices:** 6

ham and broccoli fettuccine

prep time: 30 Minutes • **start to finish:** 30 Minutes • 4 servings

8 oz uncooked fettuccine

2 cups bite-size broccoli florets

2 cups cubed cooked ham (8 oz)

1 teaspoon garlic-pepper blend

2 tablespoons chopped fresh Italian (flat-leaf) parsley

1½ cups chicken broth

1 tablespoon cornstarch

½ cup grated Parmesan cheese

1 Cook fettuccine as directed on package, adding broccoli during last 5 minutes of cooking time. Drain and return to saucepan. Stir in ham, garlic-pepper blend and parsley.

2 In small bowl, combine broth and cornstarch; add to fettuccine mixture. Cook over medium heat about 4 minutes, tossing gently, until mixture is heated through and sauce thickens slightly. Stir in cheese.

1 Serving: Calories 450; Total Fat 13g (Saturated Fat 5g; Trans Fat 0g); Cholesterol 85mg; Sodium 1870mg; Total Carbohydrate 52g (Dietary Fiber 6g); Protein 31g **Exchanges:** 3 Starch, 2 Vegetable, ½ Very Lean Meat, 2 Lean Meat, 1 Fat **Carbohydrate Choices:** 3½

Pasta Point

To get dinner on the table even faster and with fewer dishes to clean up, purchase cubed ham at your grocery store from the refrigerated packaged meat aisle.

spaghetti carbonara

prep time: 25 Minutes • **start to finish:** 25 Minutes • 6 servings

1 package (16 oz) spaghetti

1 clove garlic, finely chopped

6 slices bacon, cut into 1-inch pieces

3 pasteurized eggs, beaten, or ¾ cup fat-free egg product

1 tablespoon olive or vegetable oil

½ cup grated Parmesan cheese

½ cup grated Romano cheese

2 tablespoons chopped fresh parsley

¼ teaspoon pepper

Additional grated Parmesan cheese, if desired

Freshly ground pepper, if desired

1 Cook and drain spaghetti as directed on package; return to pan.

2 Meanwhile, in 10-inch skillet, cook garlic and bacon over medium heat, stirring occasionally, until bacon is crisp; drain.

3 In small bowl, mix eggs, oil, ½ cup Parmesan cheese, the Romano cheese, parsley and ¼ teaspoon pepper.

4 Add bacon mixture and egg mixture to hot cooked spaghetti. Cook over low heat, tossing constantly, until egg mixture coats spaghetti. Serve with additional Parmesan cheese and freshly ground pepper.

1 Serving: Calories 450; Total Fat 13g (Saturated Fat 5g; Trans Fat 0g); Cholesterol 25mg; Sodium 450mg; Total Carbohydrate 62g (Dietary Fiber 5g); Protein 22g **Exchanges:** 4 Starch, ½ Medium-Fat Meat **Carbohydrate Choices:** 4

....

Improvise

Add 2 cups chopped cooked chicken in step 4 before heating, if desired.

....

Pasta Point

Pasteurized eggs are uncooked eggs that have been heat-treated to kill bacteria that can cause food poisoning and gastrointestinal distress. Because the eggs in this recipe are not cooked, be sure to use pasteurized eggs. They can be found in the dairy case at large supermarkets. Fat-free egg product is also pasteurized.

scampi with fettuccine

prep time: 20 Minutes • **start to finish:** 20 Minutes • 4 servings

8   oz uncooked fettuccine

2   tablespoons olive or vegetable oil

1½   lb uncooked deveined peeled medium shrimp, thawed if frozen, tail and shells removed

2   medium green onions, thinly sliced (2 tablespoons)

2   cloves garlic, finely chopped

1   tablespoon chopped fresh or ½ teaspoon dried basil leaves

1   tablespoon chopped fresh parsley

2   tablespoons lemon juice

¼   teaspoon salt

1 Cook and drain fettuccine as directed on package. Meanwhile, in 10-inch skillet, heat oil over medium heat. Cook remaining ingredients in oil 2 to 3 minutes, stirring frequently, until shrimp are pink; remove from heat.

2 Toss fettuccine with shrimp mixture in skillet.

1 Serving: Calories 380; Total Fat 10g (Saturated Fat 1.5g; Trans Fat 0g); Cholesterol 290mg; Sodium 670mg; Total Carbohydrate 38g (Dietary Fiber 2g); Protein 33g **Exchanges:** 2½ Starch, 3½ Very Lean Meat, 1½ Fat **Carbohydrate Choices:** 2½

Pasta Point

Peeling and deveining shrimp is time-consuming—and unnecessary! Look for fresh or frozen shrimp that has already been peeled and deveined.

linguine with spicy red clam sauce

prep time: 10 Minutes • **start to finish:** 50 Minutes • 6 servings

1 pint shucked small clams, drained, liquid reserved

¼ cup olive or vegetable oil

3 cloves garlic, finely chopped

1 can (28 oz) Italian-style plum (Roma) tomatoes, drained, chopped

1 red jalapeño chile, seeded, finely chopped

1 tablespoon chopped fresh parsley

½ teaspoon salt

1 package (16 oz) linguine

Additional chopped fresh parsley, if desired

1 Chop clams; set aside. Heat oil in 10-inch skillet over medium-high heat. Cook garlic in oil about 3 minutes, stirring frequently, until soft. Stir in tomatoes and chile. Cook uncovered 3 minutes; stir in clam liquid. Heat to boiling; reduce heat. Simmer uncovered about 10 minutes or until slightly thickened.

2 Stir in clams, 1 tablespoon parsley and the salt. Cover and simmer about 30 minutes, stirring occasionally, until clams are tender.

3 Meanwhile, cook linguine as directed on package. Drain linguine and return to pan. Add clam sauce; toss gently until linguine is evenly coated. Sprinkle with additional parsley.

1 Serving: Calories 490; Total Fat 12g (Saturated Fat 2g; Trans Fat 0g); Cholesterol 20mg; Sodium 730mg; Total Carbohydrate 73g (Dietary Fiber 5g); Protein 23g **Exchanges:** 4 Starch, 2 Vegetable, 1 Lean Meat, 1½ Fat **Carbohydrate Choices:** 5

spaghetti with white clam sauce

prep time: 20 Minutes • **start to finish:** 20 Minutes • **4 servings**

1 package (7 oz) spaghetti

¼ cup butter or olive oil

2 cloves garlic,
   finely chopped

2 tablespoons chopped
   fresh parsley

2 cans (6.5 oz each) minced
   clams, undrained

½ cup grated
   Parmesan cheese

   Additional chopped fresh
   parsley

1 Cook and drain spaghetti as directed on package.

2 Meanwhile, in 1½-quart saucepan, melt butter over medium heat. Cook garlic in butter about 3 minutes, stirring occasionally, until light golden. Stir in 2 tablespoons parsley and the clams. Heat to boiling; reduce heat. Simmer uncovered 3 to 5 minutes.

3 In large bowl, toss spaghetti and clam sauce. Sprinkle with cheese and additional parsley.

1 Serving: Calories 480; Total Fat 18g (Saturated Fat 8g; Trans Fat 1g); Cholesterol 100mg; Sodium 410mg; Total Carbohydrate 45g (Dietary Fiber 3g); Protein 36g **Exchanges:** 3 Starch, 3 Medium-Fat Meat, ½ Fat **Carbohydrate Choices:** 3

•••

Improvise

For Linguine with White Clam Sauce and Basil, substitute linguine for the spaghetti and chopped fresh basil for the parsley.

CHAPTER 2

Skillet Dinners

asiago chicken and cavatappi

prep time: 30 Minutes • start to finish: 30 Minutes • 4 servings

1½   cups uncooked cavatappi pasta (5 oz)

¾   cup boiling water

½   cup julienne strips sun-dried tomatoes (not oil-packed)

1   lb boneless skinless chicken breasts, cut into ½-inch pieces

¼   teaspoon garlic-pepper blend

¼   teaspoon salt

2   cups frozen baby bean and carrot blend (from 1-lb bag)

¼   cup chopped fresh parsley

¼   cup shredded Asiago cheese

1 Cook and drain pasta as directed on package. While pasta is cooking, pour boiling water over tomatoes; let stand 10 minutes.

2 Meanwhile, spray 12-inch skillet with cooking spray; heat over medium heat. Cook chicken, garlic-pepper blend and salt in skillet 2 to 3 minutes, stirring constantly, until chicken is browned. Stir in tomato mixture and vegetables. Cover and cook about 5 minutes, stirring occasionally, until chicken is no longer pink in center and vegetables are crisp-tender.

3 Stir in pasta; cook and stir until thoroughly heated. Stir in parsley. Sprinkle with cheese.

1 Serving: Calories 380; Total Fat 8g (Saturated Fat 3g; Trans Fat 0g); Cholesterol 75mg; Sodium 610mg; Total Carbohydrate 41g (Dietary Fiber 5g); Protein 35g **Exchanges:** 2½ Starch, 1 Vegetable, 3½ Very Lean Meat, 1 Fat **Carbohydrate Choices:** 3

Improvise

Asiago is a semifirm Italian cheese with a rich, nutty flavor. It's a bit softer than Parmesan cheese and tastes a little smoother. Parmesan cheese is a good substitute if Asiago isn't available.

Pasta Point

Place parsley in a glass measuring cup and use kitchen scissors to quickly chop it.

bow ties with chicken and asparagus

prep time: 25 Minutes • start to finish: 25 Minutes • 6 servings (1½ cups each)

4 cups uncooked bow-tie (farfalle) pasta (8 oz)

1 lb fresh asparagus spears

1 tablespoon olive or vegetable oil

1 lb boneless skinless chicken breasts, cut into 1-inch pieces

1 package (8 oz) sliced fresh mushrooms (3 cups)

2 cloves garlic, finely chopped

1 cup chicken broth

1 tablespoon cornstarch

4 medium green onions, sliced (¼ cup)

2 tablespoons chopped fresh basil leaves

Salt, if desired

¼ cup finely shredded Parmesan cheese

1 Cook and drain pasta as directed on package, omitting salt.

2 Meanwhile, break off tough ends of asparagus as far down as stalks snap easily. Wash asparagus; cut into 1-inch pieces.

3 In 12-inch nonstick skillet, heat oil over medium-high heat. Add chicken; cook 2 minutes, stirring occasionally. Stir in asparagus, mushrooms and garlic. Cook 6 to 8 minutes, stirring occasionally, until chicken is no longer pink in center and vegetables are tender.

4 In small bowl, gradually stir broth into cornstarch. Stir in onions and basil. Stir cornstarch mixture into chicken mixture. Cook and stir 1 to 2 minutes or until thickened and bubbly. Season with salt. Toss with pasta. Sprinkle with cheese.

1 Serving: Calories 320; Total Fat 7g (Saturated Fat 2g; Trans Fat 0g); Cholesterol 50mg; Sodium 210mg; Total Carbohydrate 37g (Dietary Fiber 3g); Protein 27g **Exchanges:** 2 Starch, 1 Vegetable, 2½ Very Lean Meat, 1 Fat **Carbohydrate Choices:** 2½

cheesy southwest chicken skillet

prep time: 25 Minutes • **start to finish:** 30 Minutes • 4 servings

2 cups uncooked rotini pasta
(6 oz)

2 cups diced cooked chicken

1 pouch (9 oz) creamy
three-cheese cooking sauce

1 can (4.5 oz) diced green
chiles, undrained

1 cup shredded taco-flavored
cheese

Diced red bell pepper,
if desired

Sliced ripe olives, if desired

Tortilla chips, if desired

1 In 12-inch skillet, heat 3 cups water to boiling; add pasta. Cook 8 to 9 minutes or until pasta is tender; drain and return to skillet.

2 Add chicken, cooking sauce and chiles; heat to boiling, stirring occasionally. Sprinkle with cheese. Cover; let stand 3 to 5 minutes or until cheese is melted. Sprinkle with bell pepper, olives and tortilla chips.

1 Serving: Calories 580; Total Fat 27g (Saturated Fat 13g; Trans Fat 0g); Cholesterol 115mg; Sodium 1150mg; Total Carbohydrate 44g (Dietary Fiber 2g); Protein 40g **Exchanges:** 2½ Starch, ½ Other Carbohydrate, 2 Very Lean Meat, 1 Lean Meat, 1½ High-Fat Meat, 2 Fat **Carbohydrate Choices:** 3

Improvise

Change this dish with a different pasta shape, like penne or ziti.

Pasta Point

For convenience, purchase a rotisserie chicken and remove all the meat. One chicken will yield about 2 cups, enough for this recipe.

healthified chicken curry with couscous

prep time: 15 Minutes • **start to finish:** 20 Minutes • 6 servings

1 large onion, chopped (1 cup)

2 teaspoons curry powder

1⅓ cups water

⅔ cup uncooked whole wheat couscous

1 cup frozen sweet peas, thawed

2 cups chopped cooked chicken breast

1 large red bell pepper, chopped (1½ cups)

½ cup reduced-fat mayonnaise

3 tablespoons mango chutney

1 Lightly spray 12-inch skillet with cooking spray; heat over medium heat. Add onion; cook, stirring occasionally, until crisp-tender. Stir in curry powder; cook 1 minute longer.

2 Add water, couscous and peas; heat to boiling. Stir in remaining ingredients; return to boiling. Remove from heat. Cover; let stand 5 minutes.

1 Serving: Calories 270; Total Fat 9g (Saturated Fat 1.5g; Trans Fat 0g); Cholesterol 45mg; Sodium 210mg; Total Carbohydrate 28g (Dietary Fiber 3g); Protein 18g **Exchanges:** 1½ Starch, ½ Vegetable, 2 Very Lean Meat, 1½ Fat **Carbohydrate Choices:** 2

Improvise

The addition of golden or regular raisins—a common ingredient in curries—will increase the sweet flavor of this dish. Stir ½ cup raisins into the recipe if you like.

chicken pesto linguine

prep time: 15 Minutes • **start to finish:** 15 Minutes • **4 servings**

1 package (9 oz) refrigerated linguine

1 cup red bell pepper strips

1 cup frozen sweet peas (from 12-oz bag)

1 container (7 oz) refrigerated basil pesto

2 packages (6 oz each) refrigerated grilled chicken breast strips

1 cup crumbled Gorgonzola cheese

1 Fill 5-quart Dutch oven or saucepan two-thirds full of water; heat to boiling. Add linguine, bell pepper and peas; boil 2 to 3 minutes or until tender. Drain and return to Dutch oven.

2 Stir pesto, chicken and cheese into linguine mixture; cook over medium heat until thoroughly heated.

1 Serving : Calories 760; Total Fat 34g (Saturated Fat 11g; Trans Fat 0g); Cholesterol 95mg; Sodium 1290mg; Total Carbohydrate 70g (Dietary Fiber 6g); Protein 43g **Exchanges:** 4½ Starch, ½ Vegetable, 4 Very Lean Meat, 5½ Fat **Carbohydrate Choices:** 4½

••

Improvise

Use 2 cups chopped deli rotisserie chicken or leftover grilled chicken instead of the purchased grilled chicken breast strips.

••

Pasta Point

Gorgonzola is a mild form of blue cheese. If your family doesn't like Gorgonzola, substitute feta cheese.

rotisserie chicken and bow-tie pasta

prep time: 30 Minutes • start to finish: 30 Minutes • 4 servings

1½ cups water

1 pouch (9 oz) creamy three-cheese cooking sauce

1½ cups uncooked bow-tie (farfalle) pasta

2 cups deli rotisserie chicken cut into ½-inch pieces

¾ cup frozen sweet peas

1 teaspoon Italian seasoning

Sliced fresh basil, if desired

Shredded Parmesan cheese, if desired

1 In 10-inch skillet, heat water, cooking sauce and pasta to boiling, stirring occasionally. Reduce heat to medium; cover and simmer 8 minutes, stirring occasionally.

2 Add chicken, frozen peas and Italian seasoning. Cover; simmer 5 to 7 minutes longer or until pasta is tender and peas are bright green. Add salt and pepper to taste, if desired.

3 Remove from heat. Let stand a few minutes; sauce will thicken as it stands. Garnish with basil. Serve with Parmesan cheese.

1 Serving: Calories 310; Total Fat 10g (Saturated Fat 3g; Trans Fat 0g); Cholesterol 65mg; Sodium 550mg; Total Carbohydrate 29g (Dietary Fiber 2g); Protein 26g **Exchanges:** 1½ Starch, ½ Low-Fat Milk, 1½ Very Lean Meat, 1 Lean Meat, ½ Fat
Carbohydrate Choices: 2

Improvise

You can substitute peas with frozen broccoli or fresh asparagus. Try cooked, chopped ham in place of the rotisserie chicken.

Pasta Point

Rotisserie chicken is already cooked and seasoned and can be found near the deli section of the grocery store.

one-pot chicken ziti with artichokes and spinach

prep time: 35 Minutes • start to finish: 35 Minutes • 8 servings

4 cups water

2 cans (12 oz each) evaporated milk

1 teaspoon salt

2 cloves garlic, finely chopped

1 package (16 oz) uncooked ziti pasta

2 teaspoons cornstarch

2 cups shredded deli rotisserie chicken

1 can (14 oz) artichoke hearts, drained, coarsely chopped

1½ cups shredded Parmesan cheese

Juice of 2 medium lemons (about ⅔ cup)

2 tablespoons butter

4 cups baby spinach (5-oz package)

½ teaspoon pepper, if desired

1 In Dutch oven or saucepan, heat water, 1 can of the evaporated milk, the salt, garlic and pasta to a simmer over medium heat. Simmer 12 to 14 minutes, stirring frequently, until pasta is tender.

2 In medium bowl, beat remaining can of evaporated milk and the cornstarch; stir in chicken and artichoke hearts. Add to mixture in Dutch oven; return to simmer, and continue to simmer 1 to 3 minutes or until thickened and mixture coats back of spoon.

3 Remove from heat; stir in half of the cheese and the lemon juice. Stir until cheese melts, then add remaining cheese (reserving ¼ cup for serving, if desired) and butter; stir again.

4 Add spinach, and stir until wilted. Serve with reserved cheese and pepper.

1 Serving: Calories 540; Total Fat 16g (Saturated Fat 8g; Trans Fat 0g); Cholesterol 65mg; Sodium 1040mg; Total Carbohydrate 65g (Dietary Fiber 6g); Protein 34g **Exchanges:** 4 Starch, ½ Vegetable, 1 Very Lean Meat, 2 Lean Meat, 1½ Fat **Carbohydrate Choices:** 4

....

Improvise

Baby kale or Swiss chard makes a great substitution for the spinach in this recipe.

....

Pasta Point

Be sure to stir! The only way to mess up this easy dinner is to neglect the spoon.

fettuccine with chicken and vegetables

prep time: 20 Minutes • start to finish: 20 Minutes • 4 servings

1 package (9 oz) refrigerated fettuccine

2 cups fresh small broccoli florets

½ cup Italian dressing

1 lb uncooked chicken breast strips for stir-fry

1 medium red onion, cut into thin wedges

¼ teaspoon garlic-pepper blend

½ cup sliced drained roasted red bell peppers (from a jar)

Shredded Parmesan cheese, if desired

1 Cook fettuccine and broccoli together as directed on fettuccine package. Drain and return to saucepan. Toss with 2 tablespoons of the dressing. Cover to keep warm.

2 In 12-inch nonstick skillet, heat 2 tablespoons of the dressing over medium-high heat. Cook chicken, onion and garlic-pepper blend in dressing 4 to 6 minutes, stirring occasionally, until chicken is no longer pink in center.

3 Stir roasted peppers and remaining ¼ cup dressing into chicken mixture. Cook 2 to 3 minutes, stirring occasionally, until warm. Serve chicken mixture over fettuccine and broccoli. Serve with cheese.

1 Serving: Calories 460; Total Fat 17g (Saturated Fat 2g; Trans Fat 0g); Cholesterol 75mg; Sodium 460mg; Total Carbohydrate 42g (Dietary Fiber 4g); Protein 34g **Exchanges:** 2 Starch, ½ Other Carbohydrate, 4 Very Lean Meat, 3 Fat **Carbohydrate Choices:** 3

Improvise

Boneless skinless chicken breasts, cut crosswise into ¼-inch slices, can be substituted for the stir-fry strips.

If you don't have garlic-pepper blend on hand, substitute ⅛ teaspoon each garlic powder and coarse ground black pepper.

Pasta Point

For this recipe, be sure to use Italian dressing that is not creamy style.

creamy chicken and vegetables with noodles

prep time: 20 Minutes • **start to finish:** 20 Minutes • 4 servings

5 cups uncooked medium egg noodles (10 oz)

2 cups frozen mixed vegetables (from 12-oz bag), thawed, drained

6 medium green onions, sliced (6 tablespoons)

1 container (8 oz) garden vegetable cream cheese spread

1¼ cups milk

1½ cups chopped deli rotisserie chicken (from 2-lb chicken)

½ teaspoon garlic salt

¼ teaspoon pepper

2 tablespoons French-fried onions (from 2.8-oz can), if desired

1 Cook and drain noodles as directed on package.

2 Meanwhile, spray 12-inch skillet with cooking spray; heat over medium heat. Cook mixed vegetables and green onions in skillet about 4 minutes, stirring frequently, until vegetables are crisp-tender. Stir in cream cheese and milk until blended. Stir in chicken, garlic salt and pepper; cook until hot.

3 Stir in noodles; cook until hot. Sprinkle with French-fried onions.

1 Serving: Calories 620; Total Fat 25g (Saturated Fat 13g; Trans Fat 0.5g); Cholesterol 155mg; Sodium 1130mg; Total Carbohydrate 65g (Dietary Fiber 6g); Protein 32g **Exchanges:** 3 Starch, 1 Other Carbohydrate, 1 Vegetable, 3 Medium-Fat Meat, 1½ Fat **Carbohydrate Choices:** 4

Improvise

Choose 2 cups of your family's favorite frozen vegetable to use in place of the mixed vegetables. Corn, peas or green beans would all be good choices. To quickly thaw the frozen vegetables, place in a colander or strainer; rinse with warm water until thawed. Drain well.

chicken and noodles skillet

prep time: 40 Minutes • **start to finish:** 40 Minutes • **4 servings**

1 tablespoon vegetable oil

1 lb boneless skinless chicken breasts, cut into bite-size pieces

1 medium onion, chopped (½ cup)

1 cup ready-to-eat baby-cut carrots, cut lengthwise in half

1 cup frozen broccoli cuts

1 cup uncooked egg noodles (2 oz)

1¾ cups chicken broth (from 32-oz carton)

1 can (10.75 oz) condensed cream of chicken soup

Chopped fresh parsley, if desired

1 In 12-inch nonstick skillet, heat oil over medium-high heat. Add chicken and onion; cook 6 to 8 minutes, stirring frequently, until browned and onion is just tender.

2 Stir in remaining ingredients except parsley. Heat to boiling. Reduce heat; cover and simmer 10 minutes. Uncover and simmer 5 to 8 minutes longer, stirring occasionally, until chicken is no longer pink in center and noodles are tender. Sprinkle with parsley.

1 Serving: Calories 340; Total Fat 13g (Saturated Fat 3.5g; Trans Fat 0g); Cholesterol 85mg; Sodium 1080mg; Total Carbohydrate 24g (Dietary Fiber 3g); Protein 32g **Exchanges:** 1 Starch, 2 Vegetable, 3½ Lean Meat, ½ Fat **Carbohydrate Choices:** 1½

Pasta Point

Using one 9-ounce package of frozen diced cooked chicken breasts will reduce the cooking time. Be sure to thaw the chicken first.

sausage pasta puttanesca

prep time: 15 Minutes • start to finish: 15 Minutes • 6 servings (1¼ cups each)

- 8 oz uncooked whole wheat angel hair (capellini) pasta
- 1 jar (25.5 oz) fire-roasted tomato pasta sauce
- ¼ cup coarsely chopped pitted kalamata olives
- 1 teaspoon anchovy paste
- ½ teaspoon crushed red pepper flakes
- 8 oz Italian turkey sausage links, casings removed
- 3 tablespoons small fresh basil leaves

1 Cook pasta and drain as directed on package, omitting salt and oil.

2 Meanwhile, in 2-quart saucepan, heat pasta sauce, olives, anchovy paste and pepper flakes to boiling over medium-high heat, stirring often. Reduce heat; simmer 3 minutes.

3 Generously spray 12-inch skillet with cooking spray; heat over medium-high heat. Add sausage; cook 4 minutes, stirring to crumble, until thoroughly cooked. Drain, if necessary.

4 Add sauce and cooked pasta to skillet; toss to coat. Sprinkle individual servings with basil.

1 Serving: Calories 230; Total Fat 7g (Saturated Fat 1.5g; Trans Fat 0g); Cholesterol 0mg; Sodium 700mg; Total Carbohydrate 30g (Dietary Fiber 8g); Protein 12g **Exchanges:** 1½ Starch, ½ Other Carbohydrate, 1 Medium-Fat Meat **Carbohydrate Choices:** 2

turkey florentine skillet lasagna

prep time: 15 Minutes • **start to finish:** 30 Minutes • 8 servings

12 oz ground turkey breast

1 large onion, chopped (1 cup)

1 container (16 oz) fat-free cottage cheese

1 box (9 oz) frozen chopped spinach, thawed, squeezed to drain

4 cups tomato-basil pasta sauce

10 precooked lasagna noodles (shelf stable or frozen), each about 7x3 inches

1¼ cups shredded reduced-fat Italian cheese blend

1 Spray 12-inch skillet with cooking spray; heat over medium-high heat. Add turkey and onion; cook 4 minutes, stirring frequently, until turkey is thoroughly cooked and onion is tender.

2 In food processor or blender, place cottage cheese. Cover; process until smooth.

3 Add spinach and 3 cups of the pasta sauce to turkey mixture. Cook 1 minute, stirring constantly, until thoroughly heated. Remove mixture from skillet to bowl; cover to keep warm.

4 Add remaining 1 cup pasta sauce to skillet. Top with 5 of the noodles, half of the turkey mixture, half of the cottage cheese and half of the cheese blend. Repeat with remaining noodles, turkey mixture, cottage cheese and cheese blend. Cover; cook over medium heat 8 minutes or until noodles are tender. Remove from heat; let stand 5 minutes before serving.

1 Serving: Calories 310; Total Fat 4.5g (Saturated Fat 2.5g; Trans Fat 0g); Cholesterol 40mg; Sodium 720mg; Total Carbohydrate 39g (Dietary Fiber 4g); Protein 28g
Exchanges: ½ Starch, 2 Other Carbohydrate, 1 Vegetable, 3 Very Lean Meat, ½ Medium-Fat Meat **Carbohydrate Choices:** 2½

cilantro orzo and beef

prep time: 30 Minutes • **start to finish:** 30 Minutes • 6 servings

3 cups beef broth (from 32-oz carton)

1½ cups uncooked orzo or rosamarina pasta (9 oz)

1 can (11 oz) vacuum-packed whole kernel corn, undrained

1 can (4.5 oz) chopped green chiles, undrained

2 teaspoons olive, canola or soybean oil

8 oz cut-up extra-lean beef for stir-fry

1 large bell pepper (any color), cut into ¼-inch strips

¼ cup chopped fresh cilantro

1 In 2-quart saucepan, mix broth, pasta, corn and chiles. Heat to boiling; reduce heat. Cover; simmer about 10 minutes or until pasta is just tender. Remove from heat. Let stand about 5 minutes or until almost all liquid is absorbed.

2 Meanwhile, spray 10-inch skillet with cooking spray. Add oil; heat over medium-high heat. Add beef and bell pepper; cook about 5 minutes, stirring occasionally, until beef is browned.

3 Stir beef mixture into pasta mixture. Stir in cilantro.

1 Serving: Calories 260; Total Fat 4.5g (Saturated Fat 1g; Trans Fat 0g); Cholesterol 20mg; Sodium 950mg; Total Carbohydrate 38g (Dietary Fiber 3g); Protein 17g **Exchanges:** 2 Starch, ½ Other Carbohydrate, 1½ Lean Meat **Carbohydrate Choices:** 2½

parmesan orzo and meatballs

prep time: 20 Minutes • **start to finish:** 20 Minutes • 4 servings

1½ cups frozen bell pepper and onion stir-fry (from 1-lb bag)

2 tablespoons Italian dressing

1¾ cups beef broth (from 32-oz carton)

1 cup uncooked orzo or rosamarina pasta (6 oz)

1 bag (10.5 oz) frozen cooked Italian meatballs (about 16 meatballs)

1 large tomato, chopped (1 cup)

2 tablespoons chopped fresh parsley

¼ cup shredded Parmesan cheese

1 In 12-inch nonstick skillet, cook stir-fry vegetables and dressing over medium-high heat 2 minutes. Stir in broth; heat to boiling. Stir pasta and meatballs into vegetables. Heat to boiling; reduce heat to low. Cover and simmer 10 minutes, stirring occasionally.

2 Stir in tomato. Cover and simmer 3 to 5 minutes or until most of the liquid has been absorbed and pasta is tender. Stir in parsley. Sprinkle with cheese.

1 Serving: Calories 480; Total Fat 23g (Saturated Fat 7g; Trans Fat 0.5g); Cholesterol 30mg; Sodium 1120mg; Total Carbohydrate 45g (Dietary Fiber 4g); Protein 23g **Exchanges:** 2½ Starch, ½ Other Carbohydrate, ½ Vegetable, 1 Lean Meat, 1 High-Fat Meat, 2 Fat **Carbohydrate Choices:** 3

chili macaroni skillet

prep time: 30 Minutes • start to finish: 30 Minutes • 5 servings

1 lb bulk pork sausage

1 box Hamburger Helper™ chili macaroni

3½ cups hot water

2 teaspoons chili powder

1 can (15 oz) pinto or dark red kidney beans, drained, rinsed

1 can (14.5 oz) diced tomatoes, undrained

1 can (11 oz) whole kernel corn with red and green peppers, drained

Shredded Cheddar cheese, if desired

Additional chili powder, if desired

1 In 12-inch skillet, cook sausage over medium-high heat, stirring occasionally, until no longer pink; drain.

2 Stir in uncooked pasta and sauce mix (from Hamburger Helper box) and remaining ingredients except cheese and additional chili powder. Heat to boiling, stirring frequently.

3 Reduce heat; cover and simmer about 10 minutes, stirring occasionally, until pasta is tender. Remove from heat. Spoon into individual serving bowls; sprinkle with cheese and additional chili powder.

1 Serving: Calories 400; Total Fat 14g (Saturated Fat 4g; Trans Fat 0g); Cholesterol 35mg; Sodium 1310mg; Total Carbohydrate 52g (Dietary Fiber 6g); Protein 17g **Exchanges:** 3 Starch, ½ Other Carbohydrate, 1 High-Fat Meat, 1 Fat **Carbohydrate Choices:** 3½

....

Improvise

Spice this dish up by using 1 pound of hot or spicy pork sausage and substituting ¼ cup cayenne pepper sauce (hot sauce) for the chili powder.

One cup of frozen corn can be substituted for the canned corn.

....

Pasta Point

You'll want to use a 12-inch skillet for this recipe because of the amount of ingredients. If you don't have a skillet that large, use a large saucepot.

one-pot pasta bolognese

prep time: 35 Minutes • start to finish: 35 Minutes • 6 servings

- 2 tablespoons olive oil
- 2 medium onions, diced (about 3 cups)
- 2 medium carrots, diced (about 1 cup)
- 1 teaspoon salt
- 1 lb lean (at least 80%) ground beef
- ¼ cup canned tomato paste
- 1 can (28 oz) fire-roasted diced tomatoes, undrained
- 1 carton (32 oz) beef broth
- ½ teaspoon crushed red pepper flakes
- 2 teaspoons Italian seasoning
- 1 package (16 oz) spaghetti
- ½ cup shredded Parmesan cheese
- ¼ cup thinly sliced fresh basil leaves

1 In Dutch oven or saucepan, heat oil over medium-high heat until hot. Cook onions, carrots and salt in oil 5 to 8 minutes or until softened. Add beef; cook 5 to 8 minutes, stirring frequently, until browned.

2 Stir in tomato paste and tomatoes. Stir in broth, pepper flakes and Italian seasoning; heat to simmering. Break pasta in half, then thoroughly rinse under cold water. Add pasta to simmering liquid, covering completely. Reduce heat to medium-low; cook 13 to 15 minutes or until pasta is soft and sauce is reduced slightly, stirring occasionally.

3 Top with cheese and basil.

1 Serving: Calories 630; Total Fat 18g (Saturated Fat 6g; Trans Fat 0.5g); Cholesterol 55mg; Sodium 1520mg; Total Carbohydrate 86g (Dietary Fiber 7g); Protein 32g
Exchanges: 2 Starch, 3 Other Carbohydrate, 2 Vegetable, 3 Lean Meat, 2 Fat
Carbohydrate Choices: 6

••

Improvise

This dish is very versatile and can be made with different shapes of pasta, like penne or fusilli.

••

Pasta Point

For an extra vegetable boost, stir in a couple of cups of spinach or baby kale just before serving.

beer-cheese kielbasa with tortellini

prep time: 30 Minutes • **start to finish:** 30 Minutes • 4 servings

1 package (9 oz) refrigerated three cheese–filled tortellini

¾ cup water

⅓ cup all-purpose flour

1 cup light beer (from 12-oz bottle)

⅓ cup sliced green onions with tops

3 tablespoons chili sauce

2 teaspoons dry mustard

½ teaspoon salt

1 package (14 oz) cooked kielbasa or other smoked sausage, cut diagonally into 1-inch-thick slices

1½ cups shredded Cheddar cheese

2 tablespoons diced roasted red bell peppers (from a jar)

1 Fill 12-inch nonstick skillet half full with water (about 6 cups). Heat to boiling. Add tortellini; cook uncovered for minimum time as directed on package, stirring occasionally. Drain.

2 In 1-cup measuring cup, stir ¾ cup water and the flour with whisk until smooth; pour into same skillet. Stir in beer, green onions, chili sauce, mustard and salt. Heat to boiling. Reduce heat; simmer uncovered 1 minute, stirring constantly, until thickened.

3 Gently fold in tortellini and kielbasa. Cover; cook over medium-low heat about 5 minutes or until kielbasa is hot.

4 Fold in cheese, ½ cup at a time, until melted. Remove from heat; garnish with roasted peppers.

1 Serving: Calories 740; Total Fat 46g (Saturated Fat 21g; Trans Fat 1g); Cholesterol 125mg; Sodium 1950mg; Total Carbohydrate 46g (Dietary Fiber 3g); Protein 32g
Exchanges: 2 Starch, 1 Other Carbohydrate, 4 High-Fat Meat, 2½ Fat
Carbohydrate Choices: 3

Improvise

Add 1 cup frozen sweet peas with the kielbasa in step 3.

Mix-and-Match Pasta and Sauce

A perennial favorite, pasta lends itself to a variety of wonderful meal combinations. Because there are so many shapes and sizes, often it is difficult to choose a sauce that will complement the pasta that you are using. While you can serve any sauce with any pasta, a heartier sauce will usually partner well with larger pasta, and lighter sauces work well with thinner or smaller pasta. Here are some combinations that you might like to try.

HEARTY SAUCES

Bolognese

Italian Tomato Sauce

Short Rib Sausage Ragu

    Penne

    Mostaccioli

    Rotini or Rotelle

    Fettuccine

Mostaccioli

Rotini or Rotelle

Fettuccine

Bolognese

Penne

LIGHTER SAUCES

Marinara Sauce

Creamy Tomato-Vodka Sauce

Arrabbiata Pasta Sauce

Puttanesca

    Spaghetti

    Linguini

    Mezze Penne

    Farfalle (Bow Ties)

Orecchiette

Farfalle (Bow Ties)

Tortellini

Pesto Sauce

Mezze Penne

Spaghetti

fettuccine with italian sausage and olive sauce

prep time: 30 Minutes • start to finish: 30 Minutes • 4 servings

1   lb bulk Italian pork sausage

2   cans (14.5 oz each) diced tomatoes with basil, garlic and oregano, undrained

1   can (8 oz) tomato sauce

½   cup assorted small pitted olives

1   package (9 oz) refrigerated fettuccine

½   cup shredded Parmesan cheese

1 In 12-inch skillet, cook sausage over medium-high heat 5 to 7 minutes, stirring occasionally, until no longer pink; drain if necessary.

2 Stir tomatoes, tomato sauce and olives in with sausage. Reduce heat to low. Cover; cook 10 to 15 minutes, stirring occasionally, to blend flavors.

3 Meanwhile, cook and drain fettuccine as directed on package. Serve sauce over fettuccine. Sprinkle with cheese.

1 Serving: Calories 610; Total Fat 29g (Saturated Fat 10g; Trans Fat 0g); Cholesterol 75mg; Sodium 2340mg; Total Carbohydrate 57g (Dietary Fiber 3g); Protein 32g **Exchanges:** 2½ Starch, 1 Other Carbohydrate, 1 Vegetable, 3 High-Fat Meat, ½ Fat
Carbohydrate Choices: 4

Improvise

Hot Italian sausage is a definite option here and would go especially well with the flavor of the olives, but if you prefer, milder sausage can certainly be used.

cajun pasta with smoked sausage

prep time: 25 Minutes • start to finish: 25 Minutes • 6 servings

8   oz uncooked fettuccine

2   tablespoons vegetable oil

1   large onion, chopped
    (1 cup)

2   medium red or green bell
    peppers, thinly sliced

3   cloves garlic,
    finely chopped

1   package (14 oz)
    smoked sausage, cut into
    ½-inch slices

1   can (28 oz) fire-roasted
    crushed tomatoes,
    undrained

1   tablespoon Cajun seasoning

½   cup heavy whipping cream

½   cup shredded
    Parmesan cheese

    Chopped fresh parsley,
    if desired

1 In Dutch oven or large saucepan, cook and drain fettuccine as directed on package; return to pan. Cover to keep warm.

2 Meanwhile, in 12-inch nonstick skillet, heat oil over medium-high heat. Cook onion, bell peppers and garlic in oil 3 to 4 minutes, stirring frequently, until vegetables are crisp-tender. Add sausage; cook 3 to 4 minutes, stirring frequently, until browned.

3 Stir tomatoes and Cajun seasoning into sausage mixture. Stir in whipping cream; cook uncovered 5 to 8 minutes, stirring occasionally, or until mixture is thickened.

4 Add sausage mixture to fettuccine in Dutch oven; toss to combine. Sprinkle with cheese and parsley.

1 Serving : Calories 560; Total Fat 35g (Saturated Fat 14g; Trans Fat 1g); Cholesterol 100mg; Sodium 1890mg; Total Carbohydrate 43g (Dietary Fiber 4g); Protein 18g **Exchanges:** 1½ Starch, 1 Other Carbohydrate, 1 Vegetable, ½ Lean Meat, 1 High-Fat Meat, 5 Fat **Carbohydrate Choices:** 3

Improvise

For extra spice, add 1 teaspoon red pepper sauce.

Pasta Point

After tossing the fettuccine and sausage mixture, transfer to a 13x9-inch (3-quart) glass baking dish. Cover and refrigerate until ready to bake. Bake in 375°F oven 30 to 40 minutes or until thoroughly heated.

butternut squash, sausage and bow ties

prep time: 45 Minutes • start to finish: 45 Minutes • 4 servings

2½ cups uncooked bow-tie (farfalle) pasta (6 oz)

12 oz pork breakfast sausage links, cut into 1-inch pieces

3 tablespoons olive oil

1 medium butternut squash, peeled, cut into ½- to ¾-inch pieces (4 cups)

½ cup sliced green onions (½-inch pieces)

1 teaspoon sugar

½ teaspoon salt

½ teaspoon dried marjoram leaves

¼ teaspoon dry mustard

1 Cook and drain pasta as directed on package; return to pan. Cover to keep warm.

2 Meanwhile, in 12-inch nonstick skillet, cook sausage as directed on package. Remove sausage and drippings from skillet; discard drippings.

3 Add 2 tablespoons of the oil to same skillet. Heat over medium-low heat until hot. Add squash; cover and cook 10 minutes or until almost tender, stirring occasionally.

4 Add onions; cover and cook 3 to 5 minutes or until squash is fork-tender, stirring occasionally.

5 Add cooked sausage, cooked pasta, sugar, salt, marjoram, mustard and remaining 1 tablespoon oil; mix well. Cook 3 to 5 minutes or until thoroughly heated, stirring occasionally.

1 Serving: Calories 470; Total Fat 23g (Saturated Fat 6g; Trans Fat 0g); Cholesterol 30mg; Sodium 780mg; Total Carbohydrate 51g (Dietary Fiber 4g); Protein 15g **Exchanges:** 3½ Starch, 3½ Other Carbohydrate, ½ Medium-Fat Meat, 3½ Fat **Carbohydrate Choices:** 3½

Pasta Points

Butternut squash is shaped like a peanut; it has a smooth shell that ranges in color from yellow to tan. The orange-colored flesh is very sweet and rich.

Winter squash are available in many varieties besides butternut and are all excellent sources of vitamin A and good sources of dietary fiber.

Improvise

To make this a meatless meal, omit the sausage. Add 2 cups of chopped cabbage or winter greens, such as Swiss chard, kale or radicchio, to the skillet with the onions in step 4. Cook as directed. Just before serving, sprinkle each serving with freshly ground black pepper and grated Romano cheese.

italian sausage with tomatoes and penne

prep time: 25 Minutes • **start to finish:** 25 Minutes • **4 servings**

3 cups uncooked penne pasta (9 oz)

1 lb uncooked Italian sausage links, cut crosswise into ¼-inch slices

½ cup beef broth (from 32-oz carton)

1 medium yellow summer squash, cut in half lengthwise, then cut crosswise into ¼-inch slices

2 cups grape or cherry tomatoes, halved lengthwise

6 green onions, cut into ½-inch pieces

2 tablespoons olive oil

Shaved Parmesan cheese, if desired

1 Cook and drain pasta as directed on package.

2 Meanwhile, spray 12-inch skillet with cooking spray; heat over medium-high heat. Cook sausage in skillet 4 to 6 minutes, stirring frequently, until browned. Stir in broth; reduce heat to medium. Cover and cook 5 minutes.

3 Stir in squash, tomatoes and 2 tablespoons of the basil. Heat to boiling; reduce heat to low. Cover and simmer 5 minutes, stirring occasionally. Stir in onions. Simmer uncovered 1 minute.

4 Toss pasta, oil and remaining 2 tablespoons basil. Divide pasta among individual bowls. Top with sausage mixture and cheese.

1 Serving: Calories 490; Total Fat 31g (Saturated Fat 9g; Trans Fat 0g); Cholesterol 70mg; Sodium 1140mg; Total Carbohydrate 30g (Dietary Fiber 3g); Protein 21g **Exchanges:** 1 Starch, ½ Other Carbohydrate, 2 Vegetable, 2 High-Fat Meat, 3 Fat
Carbohydrate Choices: 2

stove-top lasagna

prep time: **30 Minutes** • start to finish: **30 Minutes** • **6 servings**

1 lb bulk Italian pork sausage

1 medium onion, halved, sliced (½ cup)

1 jar (26 to 30 oz) chunky tomato pasta sauce (any variety)

1 jar (4.5 oz) sliced mushrooms, drained

1 medium green bell pepper, cut into thin bite-size strips

3 cups uncooked mini lasagna (mafalda) noodles or medium egg noodles (6 oz)

2½ cups water

½ teaspoon Italian seasoning

1 cup shredded Italian-style cheese blend or mozzarella cheese

Chopped fresh basil, if desired

1 In 12-inch skillet or 4-quart Dutch oven, cook sausage and onion over medium-high heat, stirring occasionally, until sausage is no longer pink; drain.

2 Stir remaining ingredients except cheese and basil into sausage. Heat to boiling, stirring occasionally.

3 Reduce heat to medium; simmer uncovered about 10 minutes or until pasta is tender. Sprinkle with cheese. Let stand 2 minutes. Garnish with basil.

1 Serving: Calories 450; Total Fat 20g (Saturated Fat 7g; Trans Fat 0g); Cholesterol 45mg; Sodium 1090mg; Total Carbohydrate 50g (Dietary Fiber 4g); Protein 18g **Exchanges:** 2 Starch, 1 Other Carbohydrate, 1 Vegetable, 1½ High-Fat Meat, 1½ Fat **Carbohydrate Choices:** 3

Improvise

Ground beef can be used for the sausage if you like a milder flavor.

salsa-pork couscous

prep time: 20 Minutes • **start to finish:** 20 Minutes • 4 servings

1½ cups uncooked couscous

1 lb pork tenderloin, thinly sliced

1 medium sweet potato, peeled, sliced into thin bite-size strips

1 cup chunky-style salsa

½ cup water

2 tablespoons honey

¼ cup chopped fresh cilantro

1 Cook couscous as directed on package.

2 Meanwhile, spray 12-inch skillet with cooking spray. Cook pork in skillet over medium heat 2 to 3 minutes, stirring occasionally, until browned.

3 Stir sweet potato, salsa, water and honey into pork. Heat to boiling; reduce heat to medium. Cover and cook 5 to 6 minutes, stirring occasionally, until potato is tender and pork is no longer pink in center. Sprinkle with cilantro. Serve pork mixture over couscous.

1 Serving: Calories 450; Total Fat 5g (Saturated Fat 1.5g; Trans Fat 0g); Cholesterol 50mg; Sodium 530mg; Total Carbohydrate 70g (Dietary Fiber 4g); Protein 31g **Exchanges:** 3½ Starch, 1 Other Carbohydrate, ½ Vegetable, 2½ Very Lean Meat, ½ Fat **Carbohydrate Choices:** 4½

Improvise

If you like, substitute 1 cup sliced (¼-inch) carrots for the sweet potato. Cook as directed until carrots are tender.

pork, broccoli and noodle skillet

prep time: 30 Minutes • start to finish: 30 Minutes • 5 servings

- **4 cups uncooked dumpling egg noodles (8 oz)**
- **1 bag (12 oz) frozen broccoli florets**
- **1 tablespoon butter**
- **1 lb pork tenderloin, cut crosswise into ¼-inch slices**
- **1 cup sliced fresh mushrooms (3 oz)**
- **1 clove garlic, finely chopped**
- **1 jar (12 oz) mushroom gravy**
- **1 tablespoon Worcestershire sauce**

Improvise

Use 2¾ cups mini lasagna (mafalda) noodles as a substitute for the egg noodles.

1 Cook noodles as directed on package, adding broccoli during last 3 to 5 minutes of cooking time. Cook until noodles and broccoli are tender. Drain and return to pan. Cover to keep warm.

2 In 12-inch nonstick skillet, melt butter over medium-high heat. Add pork; cook 3 to 5 minutes, stirring frequently, until browned. Add mushrooms and garlic; cook 2 to 4 minutes, stirring frequently, until mushrooms are tender.

3 Stir in gravy and Worcestershire sauce. Cook over medium-high heat, stirring frequently, until bubbly and thickened. Add pork mixture to noodles and broccoli; toss gently to coat.

1 Serving: Calories 390; Total Fat 17g (Saturated Fat 6g; Trans Fat 0.5g); Cholesterol 80mg; Sodium 710mg; Total Carbohydrate 34g (Dietary Fiber 4g); Protein 25g
Exchanges: 2 Starch, ½ Vegetable, 2½ Lean Meat, 1½ Fat **Carbohydrate Choices:** 2

pasta with prosciutto and asiago cheese

prep time: 25 Minutes • start to finish: 25 Minutes • 4 servings

2 cups uncooked fusilli pasta (6 oz)

2 tablespoons olive or vegetable oil

1 package (8 oz) sliced fresh mushrooms (3 cups)

6 medium green onions, cut into ½-inch pieces

1 medium red bell pepper, coarsely chopped (1 cup)

1 clove garlic, finely chopped

1 package (3 oz) thinly sliced prosciutto, cut into thin strips

1 tablespoon chopped fresh or ½ teaspoon dried basil leaves

2 teaspoons chopped fresh or ¼ teaspoon dried oregano leaves

¼ teaspoon salt

¼ cup shredded Asiago cheese

1 Cook and drain pasta as directed on package.

2 Meanwhile, in 10-inch nonstick skillet, heat 1 tablespoon of the oil over medium-high heat. Cook mushrooms, onions, bell pepper and garlic in oil 2 to 3 minutes, stirring occasionally, until vegetables are tender. Stir in prosciutto, basil, oregano and salt.

3 In large bowl, toss pasta, vegetable mixture and remaining 1 tablespoon oil. Sprinkle with cheese.

1 Serving: Calories 320; Total Fat 12g (Saturated Fat 3g; Trans Fat 0g); Cholesterol 20mg; Sodium 560mg; Total Carbohydrate 39g (Dietary Fiber 4g); Protein 15g **Exchanges:** 2 Starch, 2 Vegetable, 1 Lean Meat, 1½ Fat **Carbohydrate Choices:** 2½

• •

Improvise

If you like, half of a 6-ounce package of thinly sliced cooked ham can be substituted for the prosciutto.

bacon-spinach fettuccine

prep time: 30 Minutes • **start to finish:** 30 Minutes • 8 servings

1 package (16 oz) fettuccine

1 box (9 oz) frozen chopped spinach

1 tablespoon butter

1 clove garlic, finely chopped

2 oz fat-free cream cheese, cut into cubes

¾ cup reduced-sodium chicken broth

3 tablespoons all-purpose flour

¾ cup grated Romano cheese

¾ cup fat-free half-and-half

1 teaspoon salt

½ teaspoon pepper

8 slices center-cut bacon, crisply cooked, crumbled (about 1 cup)

1 In Dutch oven or saucepan, cook fettuccine as directed on package, omitting salt and oil. Drain, reserving ½ cup cooking water. Return fettuccine to pan; cover to keep warm. Meanwhile, cook frozen spinach as directed on box; squeeze dry.

2 In 12-inch nonstick skillet, melt butter over medium-high heat. Add garlic; cook and stir 30 seconds. Add reserved cooking water and the cream cheese, stirring with whisk until smooth.

3 In small bowl, stir broth and flour with whisk until smooth. Add flour mixture to skillet, stirring with whisk until blended. Heat to boiling; cook 2 minutes, stirring constantly, until mixture thickens. Remove from heat. Add Romano cheese; stir until smooth. Add half-and-half, salt and pepper. Stir in spinach.

4 Add spinach mixture to fettuccine in Dutch oven; toss to coat. Divide mixture among 8 bowls; sprinkle evenly with bacon.

1 Serving: Calories 360; Total Fat 9g (Saturated Fat 4g; Trans Fat 0g); Cholesterol 25mg; Sodium 770mg; Total Carbohydrate 52g (Dietary Fiber 3g); Protein 18g **Exchanges:** 3½ Starch, 1 Medium-Fat Meat, ½ Fat **Carbohydrate Choices:** 3½

creole shrimp pasta

prep time: 30 Minutes • start to finish: 30 Minutes • 4 servings

1¼ cups uncooked orzo or rosamarina pasta (8 oz)

2 tablespoons olive oil

1 large onion, chopped (1 cup)

2 medium stalks celery, thinly sliced (1 cup)

2 small yellow or green bell peppers or 1 of each, chopped (1 cup)

3 large cloves garlic, finely chopped

1 can (28 oz) diced tomatoes, undrained

2 teaspoons Cajun seasoning

1 lb uncooked medium shrimp, peeled (tail shells removed), deveined

Chopped fresh parsley, if desired

1 Cook and drain orzo as directed on package.

2 Meanwhile, in 12-inch nonstick skillet, heat oil over medium-high heat. Cook onion and celery in oil 3 to 5 minutes, stirring frequently, until vegetables begin to soften. Add bell peppers; cook 2 to 3 minutes. Add garlic; cook 30 seconds or until fragrant.

3 Stir in tomatoes and Cajun seasoning. Heat to boiling. Add shrimp. Cook and stir over medium-high heat until shrimp are pink and vegetables are crisp-tender.

4 To serve, spoon ¾ cup orzo into each of 4 shallow bowls; top each with 1½ cups shrimp mixture. Garnish with parsley.

1 Serving: Calories 460; Total Fat 9g (Saturated Fat 1.5g; Trans Fat 0g); Cholesterol 160mg; Sodium 1430mg; Total Carbohydrate 64g (Dietary Fiber 6g); Protein 29g **Exchanges:** 3½ Starch, ½ Other Carbohydrate, 1 Vegetable, 2½ Very Lean Meat, 1 Fat **Carbohydrate Choices:** 4

Improvise

If you don't have Cajun seasoning, substitute 1 to 1½ teaspoons dried thyme leaves and ½ teaspoon red pepper sauce.

Orzo, tiny rice-shaped pasta, is a nice alternative to the traditional rice served with shrimp Creole. Feel free to substitute cooked long-grain white rice, if you prefer.

Pasta Pairing

Serve this Louisiana favorite with warm biscuits, cold butter and a large bottle of red pepper sauce.

lemon shrimp fettuccine

prep time: 20 Minutes • **start to finish:** 20 Minutes • 4 servings

- 8 oz uncooked whole-grain or spinach fettuccine
- 2 teaspoons olive oil
- 4 cloves garlic, finely chopped
- 1 lb uncooked medium shrimp, peeled (tails left on, if desired), deveined
- 1 cup reduced-sodium chicken broth
- 1 cup frozen sweet peas (from 12-oz bag), thawed
- 2 medium plum (Roma) tomatoes, finely chopped
- 1 teaspoon grated lemon peel
- ½ teaspoon ground nutmeg
- ¼ teaspoon salt
- 2 teaspoons chopped fresh Italian (flat-leaf) parsley
- 4 slices whole-grain baguette French bread, if desired

1 In Dutch oven or saucepan, cook fettuccine as directed on package, omitting salt and oil. Drain and return to Dutch oven; cover to keep warm.

2 Meanwhile, in 12-inch skillet, heat oil over medium heat. Add garlic; cook and stir 30 seconds. Add shrimp, broth and peas. Cook 3 to 4 minutes, stirring constantly, until shrimp are pink and peas are hot. Stir in tomatoes, lemon peel, nutmeg and salt.

3 Add shrimp mixture to fettuccine in Dutch oven; toss and heat through. Sprinkle with parsley. Serve with baguette slices.

1 Serving: Calories 370; Total Fat 5g (Saturated Fat 0.5g; Trans Fat 0g); Cholesterol 175mg; Sodium 1100mg; Total Carbohydrate 51g (Dietary Fiber 6g); Protein 30g **Exchanges:** 2½ Starch, ½ Other Carbohydrate, 1 Vegetable, 3 Very Lean Meat, ½ Fat **Carbohydrate Choices:** 3½

japanese shrimp and soba noodles

prep time: **30 Minutes** • start to finish: **30 Minutes** • **4 servings**

8 oz uncooked soba (buckwheat) noodles

1 tablespoon vegetable oil

1 lb uncooked medium or large shrimp, peeled, deveined

2 cloves garlic, finely chopped

1 tablespoon finely chopped gingerroot

1½ cups ready-to-eat baby-cut carrots, cut lengthwise in half

8 oz fresh green beans, halved

1¾ cups chicken broth

2 tablespoons soy sauce

1 teaspoon sugar

1 tablespoon lemon juice

1 teaspoon cornstarch

1 Cook and drain noodles as directed on package.

2 Meanwhile, heat 12-inch nonstick skillet over medium-high heat. Add oil; rotate skillet to coat bottom. Add shrimp, garlic and gingerroot; cook and stir about 3 minutes or until shrimp are pink. Remove from skillet.

3 Add carrots, green beans, 1 cup of the broth, the soy sauce and sugar to skillet. Heat to boiling. Cover and cook over medium heat 4 to 6 minutes, stirring occasionally, until vegetables are crisp-tender.

4 Stir in shrimp and lemon juice. Mix cornstarch and remaining ¾ cup broth until smooth; stir into shrimp mixture. Heat to boiling, stirring constantly. Boil and stir 1 minute. Divide noodles among 4 bowls. Top with shrimp mixture.

1 Serving: Calories 350; Total Fat 4.5g (Saturated Fat 0.5g; Trans Fat 0g); Cholesterol 155mg; Sodium 1190mg; Total Carbohydrate 46g (Dietary Fiber 9g); Protein 30g **Exchanges:** 2½ Starch, 1 Vegetable, 3 Very Lean Meat, ½ Fat **Carbohydrate Choices:** 3

. . . .

Improvise

Need an easy substitute for soba noodles? Use whole wheat spaghetti or ramen noodles.

. . . .

Pasta Point

Purchase shrimp already peeled and deveined. Frozen uncooked shrimp can also be used; just be sure to thaw them before cooking.

crab scampi with beer

prep time: 20 Minutes • **start to finish:** 20 Minutes • 4 servings

10	oz uncooked spinach fettuccine
¼	cup butter
5	cloves garlic, finely chopped
1	cup Boston lager–style beer
1	package (8 oz) refrigerated flake-style imitation crabmeat
½	teaspoon salt
⅔	cup chopped fresh parsley
1	tablespoon grated lemon peel

1 In Dutch oven or large saucepan, cook fettuccine as directed on package. Drain and return to Dutch oven; keep warm.

2 Meanwhile, in 8-inch skillet, melt butter over medium heat. Cook garlic in butter 2 minutes, stirring frequently. Stir in beer; cook 2 minutes. Stir in crabmeat and salt, breaking up crabmeat into bite-size pieces with spoon. Cook 3 minutes, stirring frequently, until crabmeat is heated through. Pour over fettuccine; toss with parsley and lemon peel.

1 Serving: Calories 420; Total Fat 15g (Saturated Fat 8g; Trans Fat 0g); Cholesterol 110mg; Sodium 1180mg; Total Carbohydrate 51g (Dietary Fiber 5g); Protein 18g **Exchanges:** 3½ Starch, 1 Very Lean Meat, 2½ Fat **Carbohydrate Choices:** 3½

Pasta Point

With a food processor, you can make easy work of chopping the garlic and parsley for this recipe. Otherwise, pick up a jar of chopped garlic near the produce section at your grocery store.

creamy salmon and tortellini

prep time: 25 Minutes • start to finish: 25 Minutes • 6 servings

1 package (20 oz) refrigerated cheese-filled tortellini

1 bag (12 oz) frozen sweet peas

1 container (12 oz) chive-and-onion sour cream potato topper

½ cup milk

¼ teaspoon pepper

2 cans (5 oz each) boneless skinless red salmon, well drained

¾ cup shredded Romano cheese

1 In 5-quart Dutch oven or saucepan, cook tortellini as directed on package, adding peas during last 2 minutes of cooking time. Drain; cover to keep warm.

2 In same pan, heat potato topper, milk and pepper over medium heat 2 minutes, stirring frequently. Add cooked tortellini and peas; gently toss to coat. Add salmon; gently fold into tortellini mixture just until heated through. Serve immediately, sprinkling each serving with 2 tablespoons cheese.

1 Serving: Calories 560; Total Fat 23g (Saturated Fat 13g; Trans Fat 0g); Cholesterol 120mg; Sodium 980mg; Total Carbohydrate 57g (Dietary Fiber 4g); Protein 31g
Exchanges: 3 Starch, ½ Other Carbohydrate, ½ Vegetable, 3 Lean Meat, 2½ Fat
Carbohydrate Choices: 4

Pasta Pairing

For a complete meal, serve this one-pan dish with Caesar salad and warm breadsticks.

alfredo salmon and noodles

prep time: 25 Minutes • **start to finish:** 25 Minutes • **4 servings**

3 cups uncooked wide egg noodles (6 oz)

1 package (10 oz) frozen chopped broccoli

½ cup Alfredo sauce

1 can (6 oz) skinless boneless pink salmon, drained and flaked

⅛ teaspoon pepper

1 Cook noodles as directed on package, adding broccoli during the last 4 to 5 minutes of cooking time. Drain and return to saucepan.

2 Stir in remaining ingredients. Cook over low heat 4 to 6 minutes, stirring occasionally, until hot.

1 Serving: Calories 320; Total Fat 13g (Saturated Fat 7g; Trans Fat 0g); Cholesterol 90mg; Sodium 440mg; Total Carbohydrate 33g (Dietary Fiber 3g); Protein 16g **Exchanges:** 2 Starch, ½ Vegetable, 1½ High-Fat Meat **Carbohydrate Choices:** 2

Improvise

You can substitute a 6-ounce can of water-packed tuna, drained, for the salmon.

linguine with tuna and tomatoes

prep time: 20 Minutes • start to finish: 20 Minutes • 4 servings

8 oz uncooked linguine

½ cup crumbled feta cheese

2 cups cherry tomatoes, quartered, or coarsely chopped tomatoes

1 can (12 oz) solid white tuna in water, drained, flaked

2 tablespoons chopped fresh parsley

2 tablespoons olive or canola oil

1 clove garlic, finely chopped

¼ teaspoon salt

1 Cook and drain linguine as directed on package; return to saucepan.

2 Reserve 2 tablespoons of the feta cheese for garnish. Add remaining feta cheese and remaining ingredients to linguine; toss to mix. Sprinkle with reserved feta cheese.

1 Serving: Calories 440; Total Fat 12g (Saturated Fat 3.5g; Trans Fat 0g); Cholesterol 35mg; Sodium 780mg; Total Carbohydrate 54g (Dietary Fiber 4g); Protein 30g **Exchanges:** 3 Starch, 1 Vegetable, 2½ Lean Meat, ½ Fat **Carbohydrate Choices:** 3½

Pasta Point

You can use extra-virgin olive oil in recipes such as this one where the oil is not heated. When extra-virgin olive oil is uncooked, its rich and fruity flavor really shines through.

tuna florentine

prep time: 25 Minutes • start to finish: 25 Minutes • 4 servings

1 box Tuna Helper™ creamy Parmesan

2 cups water

1⅔ cups milk

3 tablespoons butter

¼ teaspoon garlic powder

1 can (5 oz) tuna in water, drained

1 box (9 oz) frozen chopped spinach, thawed, squeezed to drain

1 cup cherry tomatoes, halved

1 tablespoon lemon juice

2 tablespoons grated Parmesan cheese

1 In 12-inch skillet, stir contents of pasta and sauce mix pouches (from Tuna Helper box), water, milk, butter and garlic powder. Heat to boiling over medium heat, stirring occasionally. Stir in tuna, spinach and tomatoes.

2 Reduce heat to medium-low. Cover; cook 13 to 15 minutes, stirring occasionally, until pasta is tender. Stir in lemon juice; sprinkle with cheese.

1 Serving: Calories 420; Total Fat 15g (Saturated Fat 8g; Trans Fat 1.5g); Cholesterol 40mg; Sodium 1410mg; Total Carbohydrate 50g (Dietary Fiber 4g); Protein 21g **Exchanges:** 3 Starch, ½ Vegetable, 1½ Lean Meat, 2 Fat **Carbohydrate Choices:** 3

Improvise

Substitute a can of salmon or shrimp for the tuna. Make sure you drain it well before adding to the dish.

tuna with angel hair pasta and dill

prep time: 20 Minutes • **start to finish:** 20 Minutes • **4 servings**

8 oz uncooked angel hair (capellini) pasta

1 teaspoon salt

1 tablespoon olive oil

1 cup diced red onion

2 medium carrots, sliced

1 can (14 oz) fat-free chicken broth with ⅓ less sodium

2 tablespoons lemon juice

2 pouches (7.06 oz each) albacore tuna

2 cups fresh sugar snap peas, halved

3 tablespoons chopped fresh dill

½ teaspoon lemon-pepper seasoning

1 Cook and drain pasta as directed on package, adding 1 teaspoon salt to cooking water; return to pan. Cover to keep warm.

2 Meanwhile, heat oil in 12-inch skillet over medium heat until hot. Add onion and carrots; cook 3 minutes, stirring frequently. Add broth and lemon juice; cook 3 to 4 minutes or until mixture boils. Reduce heat to medium-low; add tuna. Cook 2 minutes, stirring occasionally. Add sugar snap peas; cook an additional 4 to 6 minutes or until carrots and peas are crisp-tender, stirring occasionally. Stir in dill and lemon-pepper seasoning.

3 Divide pasta among individual serving bowls. Top each serving with tuna mixture.

1 Serving: Calories 420; Total Fat 6g (Saturated Fat 1g; Trans Fat 0); Cholesterol 30mg; Sodium 1420mg; Total Carbohydrate 55g (Dietary Fiber 4g); Protein 37g
Exchanges: 3 Starch, 3 Other Carbohydrate, 1 Vegetable, 3½ Very Lean Meat, 1 Fat
Carbohydrate Choices: 3½

Improvise

Use 3 teaspoons of dried dill weed in place of the fresh dill; the flavor and color of dried dill will be less intense than that of fresh dill.

Pasta Point

Albacore tuna is a high-fat tuna with a delicate flavor. It is the palest of all tuna, and only albacore may be labeled "white tuna." Albacore is also the most expensive canned tuna.

ravioli and vegetables with pesto cream

prep time: 20 Minutes • **start to finish:** 20 Minutes • **4 servings**

2   teaspoons olive or vegetable oil

8   oz fresh green beans, cut into 1½-inch pieces

½   medium yellow bell pepper, cut into ½-inch pieces (½ cup)

3   plum (Roma) tomatoes, cut into ½-inch pieces (1 cup)

½   teaspoon salt

16   oz frozen cheese-filled ravioli (from 24-oz bag)

½   cup sour cream

3   tablespoons basil pesto

2   teaspoons grated lemon peel

1 In 12-inch nonstick skillet, heat oil over medium-high heat. Add green beans and bell pepper; cook about 5 minutes, stirring frequently, until crisp-tender. Stir in tomatoes and salt. Cook 3 minutes.

2 Meanwhile, cook ravioli as directed on package. In small bowl, mix sour cream, pesto and lemon peel.

3 Drain ravioli and return to saucepan. Add vegetable mixture and sour cream mixture; toss.

1 Serving: Calories 380; Total Fat 24g (Saturated Fat 9g; Trans Fat 0g); Cholesterol 135mg; Sodium 1350mg; Total Carbohydrate 26g (Dietary Fiber 3g); Protein 16g **Exchanges:** 1½ Starch, 1 Vegetable, 1½ High-Fat Meat, 2 Fat **Carbohydrate Choices:** 2

easy italian skillet supper

prep time: 30 Minutes • **start to finish:** 30 Minutes • **4 servings**

1 can (14 oz) vegetable broth

1¼ cups uncooked orzo or rosamarina pasta (8 oz)

1 can (14.5 oz) diced tomatoes with basil, garlic and oregano, undrained

1 can (15 oz) black beans, drained, rinsed

2 cups frozen broccoli, cauliflower and carrots (from 1-lb bag)

2 tablespoons chopped fresh parsley, if desired

2 tablespoons shredded Parmesan cheese

1 In 10-inch skillet, heat broth to boiling. Stir in pasta. Return to boiling. Reduce heat to low; cover and simmer 10 to 12 minutes or until liquid is absorbed.

2 Stir in tomatoes, beans and vegetables. Cover; cook over medium heat 5 to 10 minutes, stirring occasionally, until vegetables are tender.

3 Stir in parsley; sprinkle with cheese.

1 Serving: Calories 370; Total Fat 3g (Saturated Fat 1g; Trans Fat 0g); Cholesterol 0mg; Sodium 940mg; Total Carbohydrate 67g (Dietary Fiber 16g); Protein 18g **Exchanges:** 4 Starch, 1 Vegetable, ½ Lean Meat **Carbohydrate Choices:** 4½

broccoli rabe and ravioli

prep time: 25 Minutes • **start to finish:** 25 Minutes • 4 servings

1 tablespoon olive oil

⅓ cup sliced leek (1 medium)

3 cloves garlic,
finely chopped

1 can (14 oz) reduced-sodium
beef broth

¾ cup water

¼ teaspoon crushed red
pepper flakes, if desired

5 cups coarsely chopped
broccoli rabe (rapini)

1 can (14.5 oz) stewed
tomatoes, undrained

1 package (9 oz)
refrigerated reduced-fat
cheese-filled ravioli

1 tablespoon chopped
fresh or 1 teaspoon dried
rosemary leaves, crushed

Grated Asiago or Parmesan
cheese, if desired

1 In 3-quart saucepan, heat oil over medium heat. Cook leek and garlic in oil 5 minutes. Add broth, water and pepper flakes. Heat to boiling.

2 Stir in broccoli rabe, tomatoes, ravioli and rosemary. Return to boiling; reduce heat. Cover; simmer 7 to 8 minutes or until broccoli rabe and ravioli are tender. Sprinkle individual servings with cheese.

1 Serving: Calories 240; Total Fat 7g (Saturated Fat 2g; Trans Fat 0g); Cholesterol 30mg; Sodium 650mg; Total Carbohydrate 33g (Dietary Fiber 3g); Protein 12g **Exchanges:** 1½ Starch, 2 Vegetable, ½ Lean Meat, 1 Fat **Carbohydrate Choices:** 2

Improvise

If you can't find broccoli rabe, substitute fresh broccoli florets.

Pasta Pairing

Pair this dish with pear! A juicy, ripe pear makes a great addition to this meal. Served whole or sliced, a medium pear adds 100 calories per serving.

penne with portabella mushrooms and fennel

prep time: 30 Minutes • **start to finish:** 30 Minutes • 6 servings

2½ cups uncooked penne pasta (about 8 oz)

2 tablespoons olive oil

1 package (8 oz) portabella mushrooms, halved, sliced

1 bulb fennel, trimmed, cut into 1-inch slices

2 cloves garlic, finely chopped

1 jar (24 oz) chunky tomato pasta sauce (any meatless variety)

1 can (15 oz) cannellini beans, drained

3 tablespoons chopped fresh or 1 tablespoon dried basil leaves

½ cup grated Asiago or Parmesan cheese

Fennel leaves, if desired

1 Cook and drain pasta as directed on package.

2 Meanwhile, in 10-inch skillet, heat oil over medium heat. Cook mushrooms, sliced fennel and garlic in oil 5 to 6 minutes, stirring occasionally, until fennel is crisp-tender. Stir in pasta sauce, beans and basil. Cook, stirring occasionally, until thoroughly heated.

3 Divide cooked pasta among 6 serving bowls or plates; spoon vegetable mixture evenly over pasta. Sprinkle with cheese. Garnish with fennel leaves.

1 Serving: Calories 490; Total Fat 15g (Saturated Fat 4g; Trans Fat 0g); Cholesterol 10mg; Sodium 900mg; Total Carbohydrate 73g (Dietary Fiber 8g); Protein 16g **Exchanges:** 2 Starch, 2 Other Carbohydrate, 2½ Vegetable, 1 Very Lean Meat, 2½ Fat **Carbohydrate Choices:** 5

Improvise

You can use any beans you like in this recipe. Try great northern beans, garbanzo beans or kidney beans.

Pasta Pairing

Serve with crusty French bread or whole-grain dinner rolls and a spinach salad with raspberry vinaigrette.

vegetarian italian pasta skillet dinner

prep time: 25 Minutes • **start to finish:** 25 Minutes • 2 servings

1⅓ cups frozen sausage-style
    soy protein crumbles

1 cup sliced fresh mushrooms

½ cup coarsely chopped
   onion (1 medium)

1 can (18.5 oz) ready-to-
   serve light Italian-style
   vegetable soup

¾ cup uncooked bow-tie
   (farfalle) pasta (2 oz)

2 cups fresh baby
   spinach leaves

¼ cup shredded mozzarella
   or Parmesan cheese

1 In 12-inch nonstick skillet, cook soy crumbles, mushrooms and onion over medium-high heat 4 to 6 minutes, stirring frequently, until crumbles are hot and vegetables are tender.

2 Stir in soup. Cover; heat to boiling. Stir in pasta; reduce heat to medium-low. Cover; simmer 10 minutes, stirring occasionally.

3 Add spinach; cook uncovered 3 to 5 minutes, stirring occasionally, until spinach is hot and just begins to wilt. Sprinkle with cheese.

1 Serving: Calories 340; Total Fat 7g (Saturated Fat 2.5g; Trans Fat 0g); Cholesterol 30mg; Sodium 1430mg; Total Carbohydrate 47g (Dietary Fiber 8g); Protein 23g **Exchanges:** 2 Starch, ½ Other Carbohydrate, 2 Vegetable, 2 Lean Meat **Carbohydrate Choices:** 3

• •

Improvise

If you're a meat lover, you may want to use ground beef or Italian sausage instead of soy protein crumbles.

italian parsley pesto ravioli

prep time: 25 Minutes • **start to finish:** 25 Minutes • 6 servings

1 package (20 oz) refrigerated cheese-filled ravioli

2 cups fresh Italian (flat-leaf) parsley

1 cup fresh basil leaves (from 3-oz container)

1 clove garlic

1 cup grated Parmesan cheese

¾ cup chopped walnuts

¼ cup olive oil

¼ cup reduced-sodium chicken broth

½ cup chopped drained roasted red bell peppers (from a jar)

1 Cook ravioli as directed on package, Drain and return to pan. Cover to keep warm.

2 Meanwhile, in blender or food processor, place parsley, basil, garlic, ½ cup of the cheese, ¼ cup of the walnuts, the oil and broth. Cover and blend on medium speed about 3 minutes, stopping occasionally to scrape sides, until almost smooth.

3 Add basil mixture to cooked ravioli in pan; toss to coat. To serve, spoon onto serving platter; garnish with bell peppers and the remaining ½ cup walnuts. Serve with remaining ½ cup cheese.

1 Serving: Calories 580; Total Fat 34g (Saturated Fat 11g; Trans Fat 0g); Cholesterol 65mg; Sodium 720mg; Total Carbohydrate 46g (Dietary Fiber 3g); Protein 22g **Exchanges:** 2½ Starch, 1 Vegetable, 1 Lean Meat, 1 Medium-Fat Meat, 5 Fat **Carbohydrate Choices:** 3

Pasta Point

To reduce the fat and trim the calories from this restaurant-worthy recipe, we used a little chicken broth to replace some of the oil typically found in traditional pesto. Keep the pesto from getting too salty by using reduced-sodium broth.

gorgonzola linguine with toasted walnuts

prep time: 25 Minutes • start to finish: 25 Minutes • 4 servings

8 oz uncooked linguine

1 tablespoon butter

1 clove garlic, finely chopped

1½ cups heavy whipping cream

¼ cup dry white wine or chicken broth

¼ teaspoon salt

½ cup crumbled Gorgonzola cheese

¼ cup coarsely chopped walnuts, toasted*

Freshly ground black pepper, if desired

Chopped fresh parsley, if desired

1 Cook and drain linguine as directed on package.

2 Meanwhile, in 10-inch skillet, melt butter over low heat. Cook garlic in butter, stirring occasionally, until golden. Stir in whipping cream, wine and salt. Simmer about 6 minutes, stirring constantly, until slightly thickened; remove from heat. Stir in cheese until melted.

3 In large bowl, toss linguine and sauce until well coated. Sprinkle with walnuts, pepper and parsley.

*To toast walnuts, sprinkle in ungreased skillet. Cook over medium heat 5 to 7 minutes, stirring frequently until nuts begin to brown, then stirring constantly until nuts are light brown.

1 Serving: Calories 620; Total Fat 41g (Saturated Fat 22g; Trans Fat 1g); Cholesterol 120mg; Sodium 620mg; Total Carbohydrate 50g (Dietary Fiber 4g); Protein 14g
Exchanges: 3 Starch, ½ High-Fat Meat, 7 Fat **Carbohydrate Choices:** 3

Pasta Point

To reduce the fat to about 11 grams and calories to 400 per serving, substitute evaporated fat-free milk for the whipping cream and use 2 tablespoons finely chopped walnuts.

lemon-pepper pasta and asparagus

prep time: 25 Minutes • **start to finish:** 25 Minutes • 4 servings

- 2 **cups uncooked farfalle (bow-tie) pasta (4 oz)**
- ¼ **cup olive or vegetable oil**
- 1 **medium red bell pepper, chopped (1 cup)**
- 1 **lb fresh asparagus spears, cut into 1-inch pieces**
- 1 **teaspoon grated lemon peel**
- ½ **teaspoon salt**
- ½ **teaspoon freshly ground black pepper**
- 3 **tablespoons lemon juice**
- 1 **can (15 oz) cannellini beans or 1 can (15.5 oz) navy beans, drained, rinsed**

  Additional freshly ground black pepper, if desired

....

Improvise

For a delicious change of flavor, use lime juice and peel instead of the lemon.

1 Cook and drain pasta as directed on package.

2 Meanwhile, in 12-inch skillet, heat oil over medium-high heat. Add bell pepper, asparagus, lemon peel, salt and ½ teaspoon pepper; cook, stirring occasionally, until vegetables are crisp-tender.

3 Stir lemon juice and beans into vegetable mixture. Cook until beans are hot. Add pasta; toss. Sprinkle with additional pepper.

1 Serving: Calories 400; Total Fat 15g (Saturated Fat 2g; Trans Fat 0g); Cholesterol 0mg; Sodium 420mg; Total Carbohydrate 52g (Dietary Fiber 9g); Protein 15g **Exchanges:** 3 Starch, 1 Vegetable, ½ Very Lean Meat, 2½ Fat **Carbohydrate Choices:** 3½

browned butter orecchiette with broccoli rabe

prep time: 30 Minutes • **start to finish:** 30 Minutes • 4 servings

1 lb broccoli rabe (rapini)

⅓ cup butter

1 tablespoon lemon juice

½ teaspoon salt

1 package (8.8 oz) orecchiette (tiny disk) pasta

Toasted pine nuts or chopped walnuts, if desired

Shredded Parmesan cheese, if desired

1 Cut off thick, tough, stem ends (about 1 inch) from broccoli rabe, and discard. Cut remaining stems into 1-inch pieces; place in small bowl and set aside. Cut leaves crosswise into 2-inch pieces (about 10 loosely packed cups); set aside. Cut any florets into bite-size pieces if necessary; set aside.

2 In 1-quart saucepan, heat butter over medium heat until butter is medium golden brown, stirring constantly. Watch carefully because butter can brown and then burn quickly. Stir in lemon juice and salt. Set aside.

3 Cook and drain pasta according to package directions, except add reserved broccoli rabe stems during last 5 minutes of cooking time.

4 Meanwhile, in 12-inch nonstick skillet, heat 1 tablespoon of the browned butter over medium heat until hot. Add reserved broccoli rabe leaves and florets; cook 4 to 6 minutes, stirring frequently, or until leaves are wilted. Add drained pasta and stems and remaining browned butter mixture; toss to coat. Heat until hot. Sprinkle with pine nuts and cheese.

1 Serving: Calories 450; Total Fat 17g (Saturated Fat 10g, Trans Fat 0.5g); Cholesterol 40mg; Sodium 710mg; Total Carbohydrate 61g (Dietary Fiber 6g, Sugars 3g); Protein 13g **Exchanges:** 3 ½ Starch, 1 Vegetable, 3 Fat **Carbohydrate Choices:** 4

Pasta Point

Broccoli rabe (rapini) is related to broccoli but isn't the same as regular or baby broccoli. Broccoli rabe has slender stems, is mostly leaves and has a pleasantly bitter flavor.

tagliatelle pasta with asparagus and gorgonzola sauce

prep time: 25 Minutes • **start to finish:** 25 Minutes • 4 servings

1 lb asparagus

8 oz uncooked tagliatelle pasta or fettuccine

2 tablespoons olive or vegetable oil

4 medium green onions, sliced (¼ cup)

¼ cup chopped fresh parsley

1 clove garlic, finely chopped

1 cup crumbled Gorgonzola cheese

½ teaspoon cracked black pepper

1 Snap off tough ends of asparagus spears. Cut asparagus into 1-inch pieces. Cook and drain pasta as directed on package, adding asparagus during last 5 minutes of cooking time.

2 Meanwhile, in 12-inch skillet, heat oil over medium-high heat. Cook onions, parsley and garlic in oil about 5 minutes, stirring occasionally, until onions are tender. Reduce heat to medium.

3 Add pasta, asparagus and cheese to mixture in skillet. Cook about 3 minutes, tossing gently, until cheese is melted and pasta is evenly coated. Sprinkle with pepper.

1 Serving: Calories 370; Total Fat 17g (Saturated Fat 7g; Trans Fat 0g); Cholesterol 70mg; Sodium 640mg; Total Carbohydrate 40g (Dietary Fiber 3g); Protein 15g **Exchanges:** 2 Starch, ½ Other Carbohydrate, 1 Vegetable, 1 High-Fat Meat, 1½ Fat
Carbohydrate Choices: 2½

winter veggie pasta

prep time: 25 Minutes • **start to finish:** 25 Minutes • 6 servings

8 oz uncooked whole wheat spaghetti

3 cups frozen broccoli florets (from 12-oz bag)

1 can (14.5 oz) no-salt-added diced tomatoes, drained

1 can (15 oz) cannellini beans, drained, rinsed

2 tablespoons no-salt-added tomato paste

2 cloves garlic, finely chopped

¼ teaspoon salt

¼ teaspoon pepper

2 tablespoons chopped fresh Italian (flat-leaf) parsley

¼ cup grated Parmesan cheese

1 In 4-quart Dutch oven or saucepan, cook spaghetti as directed on package, omitting salt and oil, and adding broccoli during last 3 minutes of cooking time. Drain and return to Dutch oven.

2 Stir in tomatoes, beans, tomato paste, garlic, salt and pepper; cook over medium-low heat until thoroughly heated. Stir in parsley. Sprinkle each serving with 2 teaspoons cheese.

1 Serving: Calories 290; Total Fat 2g (Saturated Fat 1g; Trans Fat 0g); Cholesterol 0mg; Sodium 360mg; Total Carbohydrate 51g (Dietary Fiber 9g); Protein 15g **Exchanges:** 3 Starch, 1 Vegetable, ½ Very Lean Meat **Carbohydrate Choices:** 3½

tomato-basil pasta primavera

prep time: 35 Minutes • **start to finish:** 35 Minutes • 6 servings

2⅓ cups uncooked whole-grain penne or mostaccioli pasta (8 oz)

2 cups frozen sugar snap peas

1 cup assorted fresh vegetables (such as red bell pepper strips, julienne carrots and 2-inch pieces fresh asparagus)

1 cup sliced zucchini or yellow summer squash

1 cup halved cherry tomatoes

½ cup reduced-sodium chicken broth

3 tablespoons all-purpose flour

¼ teaspoon salt

1¼ cups low-fat (1%) milk

¼ cup dry sherry or additional reduced-sodium chicken broth

¾ cup finely shredded Parmesan or Asiago cheese

½ cup lightly packed fresh basil leaves, coarsely chopped

4 teaspoons chopped fresh thyme or oregano leaves

Sliced green onions, if desired

1 In 4-quart Dutch oven or saucepan, cook pasta as directed on package, omitting salt and oil, and adding frozen sugar snap peas and 1 cup assorted vegetables during last 2 minutes of cooking time. Drain and return to Dutch oven. Add squash and tomatoes; cover to keep warm.

2 In 2-quart saucepan, stir broth, flour and salt with whisk until smooth. Stir in milk and sherry. Cook and stir until thickened and bubbly; cook and stir 2 minutes longer. Remove from heat; stir in cheese, basil and thyme.

3 Add herb sauce to pasta and vegetables in Dutch oven; toss gently to coat. Garnish individual servings with onions.

1 Serving: Calories 280; Total Fat 5g (Saturated Fat 3g; Trans Fat 0g); Cholesterol 10mg; Sodium 410mg; Total Carbohydrate 41g (Dietary Fiber 5g); Protein 15g **Exchanges:** 2½ Starch, 1 Vegetable, 1 Lean Meat **Carbohydrate Choices:** 3

Improvise

For a heartier version, add 2 cups cut-up cooked chicken breast with the cheese in step 2.

CHAPTER 3

Salads

turkey-chutney pasta salad

prep time: 25 Minutes • **start to finish:** 25 Minutes • 4 servings

1 box Betty Crocker Suddenly Salad Caesar salad mix

¼ cup mayonnaise

¼ cup sour cream

2 tablespoons mango chutney

2 teaspoons curry powder

2 cups cubed cooked turkey breast

¼ cup chopped cashews

2 tablespoons golden raisins

1 medium green onion, finely chopped (1 tablespoon)

¼ cup chopped fresh cilantro

1 Fill 3-quart saucepan two-thirds full of water; heat to boiling. Empty pasta mix (from Suddenly Salad box) into boiling water. Gently boil uncovered 12 minutes, stirring occasionally.

2 Meanwhile, in large bowl, stir together seasoning and crouton blend (from Suddenly Salad box), mayonnaise, sour cream, chutney and curry powder. Stir in turkey, cashews and raisins.

3 Drain pasta; rinse with cold water. Shake to drain well. Stir pasta into salad mixture. Spoon onto serving platter. Top with onion and cilantro. Serve immediately, or cover and refrigerate 1 hour to chill.

1 Serving: Calories 480; Total Fat 19g (Saturated Fat 4g; Trans Fat 0g); Cholesterol 70mg; Sodium 780mg; Total Carbohydrate 48g (Dietary Fiber 2g); Protein 28g **Exchanges:** 2½ Starch, ½ Other Carbohydrate, 3 Lean Meat, 2 Fat **Carbohydrate Choices:** 3

turkey-pasta salad

prep time: 45 Minutes • **start to finish:** 2 Hours 45 Minutes • 10 servings

SALAD

- 1 box (14.5 oz) multigrain or whole-grain rotini or rotelle pasta
- 3 cups small fresh broccoli florets
- 1½ cups cubed cooked turkey breast (8 oz)
- ½ cup dried cherries
- 1 small onion, chopped (⅓ cup)
- 1 medium stalk celery, chopped (½ cup)
- ½ cup unblanched whole almonds, toasted

DRESSING

- 1½ cups fat-free plain yogurt
- ½ cup reduced-fat mayonnaise
- 2 tablespoons Dijon mustard
- 1 tablespoon champagne vinegar, white wine vinegar or cider vinegar
- ¼ cup powdered sugar
- 1 teaspoon salt
- ½ teaspoon pepper
- ½ teaspoon poppy seed

1 Cook pasta as directed on package, omitting salt and adding broccoli for last 2 minutes of cooking time; drain. Rinse with cold water; drain.

2 In large bowl, mix pasta, broccoli and all remaining salad ingredients except almonds.

3 In medium bowl, beat dressing ingredients with whisk until smooth. Add to pasta mixture; toss to mix well. Cover; refrigerate at least 2 hours to blend flavors. Before serving, stir in almonds.

*To toast almonds, sprinkle in ungreased skillet. Cook over medium heat 5 to 7 minutes, stirring frequently until nuts begin to brown, then stirring constantly until nuts are light brown.

1 Serving: Calories 340; Total Fat 10g (Saturated Fat 1.5g; Trans Fat 0g); Cholesterol 25mg; Sodium 470mg; Total Carbohydrate 44g (Dietary Fiber 5g); Protein 19g
Exchanges: 2 Starch, ½ Other Carbohydrate, 1 Vegetable, 1½ Lean Meat, 1 Fat
Carbohydrate Choices: 3

Improvise

Dried cranberries can be substituted for the cherries—also, if you really like poppy seed, go ahead and stir in a little extra.

Pasta Point

If the salad is a bit dry, just stir in 1 to 2 tablespoons fat-free (skim) milk before serving.

chicken-gorgonzola pasta salad

prep time: 30 Minutes • start to finish: 30 Minutes • 12 servings

7 cups uncooked radiatore (nuggets) pasta (about 19 oz)

4½ cups cubed cooked chicken breast (about 1¼ lb)

1 package (2.1 oz) refrigerated precooked bacon (about 15 slices), cut into small pieces

1 can (14.5 oz) fire-roasted diced tomatoes, drained

2 cups lightly packed fresh baby spinach leaves

1 jar (16 oz) refrigerated ranch dressing

1 cup crumbled Gorgonzola cheese

Bibb lettuce, if desired

1 Cook and drain pasta as directed on package. Rinse with cold water; drain.

2 In large bowl, mix chicken, bacon, tomatoes, spinach and cooked pasta. Pour dressing over mixture; toss until coated. Fold in cheese.

3 Line serving bowl with lettuce; spoon salad into lettuce-lined bowl.

1 Serving: Calories 630; Total Fat 29g (Saturated Fat 6g; Trans Fat 0g); Cholesterol 70mg; Sodium 590mg; Total Carbohydrate 62g (Dietary Fiber 4g); Protein 30g **Exchanges:** 4 Starch, 2½ Lean Meat, 4 Fat **Carbohydrate Choices:** 4

. . . .

Improvise

You can use cut-up deli rotisserie chicken for the cooked chicken breast. You'll need a 2- to 2½-lb chicken for 4½ cups.

orzo with chicken and fresh herbs

prep time: 25 Minutes • start to finish: 25 Minutes • 4 servings

½ cup uncooked orzo or rosamarina pasta (about 3½ oz)

1 pint (2 cups) cherry or grape tomatoes, halved

2 cloves garlic, finely chopped

¼ cup olive oil

3 tablespoons white wine vinegar

½ teaspoon salt

⅛ teaspoon pepper

3 tablespoons chopped fresh basil, oregano, marjoram or thyme leaves (or a combination)

2 cups cut-up cooked chicken

1 cup small fresh mozzarella cheese balls (about 6 oz)

4 large leaves butter lettuce

1 Cook and drain pasta as directed on package. Rinse with cold water; drain.

2 In large bowl, mix tomatoes, garlic, oil, vinegar, salt, pepper and herbs. Add chicken, cheese and cooked pasta; toss until evenly coated. To serve, spoon 1¼ cups salad onto each lettuce leaf.

1 Serving: Calories 490; Total Fat 28g (Saturated Fat 9g; Trans Fat 0g); Cholesterol 85mg; Sodium 580mg; Total Carbohydrate 25g (Dietary Fiber 2g); Protein 35g **Exchanges:** 1½ Starch, 1 Vegetable, 4 Lean Meat, 3 Fat **Carbohydrate Choices:** 1½

Pasta Point

This recipe can easily be doubled.

caribbean jerk chicken and pasta salad

prep time: 25 Minutes • **start to finish:** 1 Hour 25 Minutes • **6 servings**

1 box Betty Crocker Suddenly Salad chipotle ranch salad mix

⅓ cup mayonnaise

1 tablespoon packed brown sugar

1 tablespoon lime juice

1 teaspoon grated gingerroot

½ teaspoon crushed red pepper flakes

2 packages (6 oz each) refrigerated grilled chicken strips, chopped

1½ cups chopped fresh pineapple

3 medium green onions, sliced (3 tablespoons)

2 teaspoons chopped fresh cilantro

1 Fill 3-quart saucepan two-thirds full of water; heat to boiling. Empty pasta mix (from Suddenly Salad box) into boiling water. Gently boil uncovered 15 minutes, stirring occasionally.

2 Meanwhile, in large bowl, stir together seasoning mix (from Suddenly Salad box), mayonnaise, brown sugar, lime juice, gingerroot and pepper flakes. Stir in chicken, pineapple, onions and cilantro.

3 Drain pasta; rinse with cold water. Shake to drain well. Stir pasta into salad mixture. Cover; refrigerate 1 hour to chill. Stir before serving.

1 Serving: Calories 300; Total Fat 13g (Saturated Fat 2g; Trans Fat 0g); Cholesterol 40mg; Sodium 670mg; Total Carbohydrate 30g (Dietary Fiber 1g); Protein 18g **Exchanges:** 1½ Starch, ½ Other Carbohydrate, 2 Lean Meat, 1 Fat **Carbohydrate Choices:** 2

chicken-thyme pasta salad

prep time: 25 Minutes • start to finish: 4 Hours 25 Minutes • 8 servings

3 cups uncooked penne pasta (9 oz)

4 cups cubed cooked chicken

2 cups seedless red grapes, halved

2 medium stalks celery, sliced (1 cup)

⅓ cup chopped onion

3 tablespoons olive or vegetable oil

2 tablespoons chopped fresh or 2 teaspoons dried thyme leaves, crushed

1¼ cups mayonnaise or salad dressing

1 tablespoon milk

1 tablespoon honey

1 tablespoon coarse-grained mustard

1 teaspoon salt

1 cup chopped walnuts, toasted*

1 Cook and drain pasta as directed on package. Rinse with cold water; drain.

2 In very large (4-quart) bowl, mix pasta, chicken, grapes, celery and onion. In small bowl, mix oil and 1 tablespoon of the fresh thyme (or 1 teaspoon of the dried thyme). Pour over chicken mixture; toss to coat.

3 In small bowl, mix mayonnaise, milk, honey, mustard, salt and remaining thyme. Cover chicken mixture and mayonnaise mixture separately; refrigerate at least 4 hours but no longer than 24 hours.

4 Up to 2 hours before serving, toss chicken mixture and mayonnaise mixture. Cover; refrigerate. Just before serving, stir in ¾ cup of the walnuts. Sprinkle salad with remaining walnuts.

*To toast walnuts, sprinkle in ungreased skillet. Cook over medium heat 5 to 7 minutes, stirring frequently until nuts begin to brown, then stirring constantly until nuts are light brown.

1 Serving: Calories 690; Total Fat 46g (Saturated Fat 7g; Trans Fat 0g); Cholesterol 80mg; Sodium 600mg; Total Carbohydrate 41g (Dietary Fiber 4g); Protein 29g **Exchanges:** 2 Starch, 1 Fruit, 3 Medium-Fat Meat, 5½ Fat **Carbohydrate Choices:** 3

. . . .

Improvise

Substitute cooked turkey for the chicken and fresh basil for the thyme.

. . . .

Pasta Point

You'll need about 2 pounds of uncooked boneless skinless chicken breasts, which equals 4 cups cubed cooked chicken, to make this dish. Cook them however you want, or buy deli rotisserie chicken.

chipotle ranch chicken and pasta salad

prep time: 20 minutes • **start to finish:** 20 minutes • **4 servings**

1 box Betty Crocker Suddenly Salad chipotle ranch salad mix

½ cup frozen corn

3 tablespoons milk

⅓ cup mayonnaise

2 cups cubed cooked chicken

½ cup coarsely chopped tomato

4 medium green onions, sliced (¼ cup)

Lime wedges, if desired

1 Fill 3-quart saucepan two-thirds full of water; heat to boiling. Empty pasta mix (from Suddenly Salad box) into boiling water. Gently boil uncovered 15 minutes, stirring occasionally and adding corn during last 3 minutes of cooking time.

2 Meanwhile, in large bowl, stir together seasoning mix (from Suddenly Salad box) and milk until blended. Stir in mayonnaise.

3 Drain pasta with corn; rinse with cold water. Shake to drain well. Stir pasta with corn, chicken, tomato and onions into bowl with dressing. Serve with lime wedges.

1 Serving: Calories 420; Total Fat 19g (Saturated Fat 3g; Trans Fat 0g); Cholesterol 65mg; Sodium 560mg; Total Carbohydrate 36g (Dietary Fiber 2g); Protein 27g **Exchanges:** 2 Starch, ½ Other Carbohydrate, 3 Lean Meat, 1½ Fat **Carbohydrate Choices:** 2½

Improvise

For a lighter dressing, substitute reduced-fat mayonnaise.

lemon-chicken pasta salad

prep time: 25 Minutes • **start to finish:** 25 Minutes • **4 servings**

1 box Betty Crocker Suddenly Salad ranch & bacon salad mix

1 cup mayonnaise

2 teaspoons grated lemon peel

2 tablespoons lemon juice

2 cups cubed cooked chicken

1½ cups fresh snow pea pods, strings removed, cut diagonally into ½-inch pieces

½ cup sliced almonds

Lettuce leaves, if desired

1 Fill 3-quart saucepan two-thirds full of water; heat to boiling. Empty pasta mix (from Suddenly Salad box) into boiling water. Gently boil uncovered 12 minutes, stirring occasionally.

2 Meanwhile, in large bowl, mix contents of seasoning pouch (from Suddenly Salad box), mayonnaise, lemon peel and lemon juice.

3 Drain pasta; rinse with cold water. Shake to drain well. Stir cooked pasta, chicken, pea pods and almonds into mayonnaise mixture. Serve immediately in lettuce-lined bowl, or cover and refrigerate until serving time.

1 Serving: Calories 800; Total Fat 56g (Saturated Fat 9g; Trans Fat 0g); Cholesterol 80mg; Sodium 800mg; Total Carbohydrate 43g (Dietary Fiber 3g); Protein 31g
Exchanges: 1½ Starch, 1 Other Carbohydrate, 1 Vegetable, 3½ Lean Meat, 9 Fat
Carbohydrate Choices: 3

Pasta Point

Make this salad up to 24 hours before serving and store in the refrigerator. If needed, stir in a few drops of milk to make it creamy again.

confetti chicken 'n couscous salad

prep time: 25 Minutes • **start to finish:** 25 Minutes • **6 servings**

SALAD

- 1 box (10 oz) couscous
- 2 cups chopped cooked chicken
- 2 medium carrots, finely chopped (1½ cups)
- 1 medium red bell pepper, finely chopped (1 cup)
- ½ cup chopped fresh chives

DRESSING

- ½ cup olive or vegetable oil
- ⅓ cup lemon juice
- ⅔ cup grated Parmesan cheese
- 1½ teaspoons salt

1 Cook couscous as directed on box.

2 In large bowl, mix chicken, carrots, bell pepper and chives. Add cooked couscous; fluff with fork until well mixed. Cool slightly.

3 In tightly covered container, shake dressing ingredients. Pour over salad; toss gently to coat. Serve immediately.

1 Serving: Calories 490; Total Fat 25g (Saturated Fat 5g; Trans Fat 0g); Cholesterol 50mg; Sodium 820mg; Total Carbohydrate 41g (Dietary Fiber 3g); Protein 24g **Exchanges:** 2½ Starch, 1 Vegetable, 2 Lean Meat, 3½ Fat **Carbohydrate Choices:** 3

Pasta Point

If you're going to make this recipe ahead of time and store it in the refrigerator, you may need to add a little bit more olive oil and/or lemon juice when ready to serve. When made ahead, the couscous will absorb these ingredients over time.

ultimate chicken-pasta salad

prep time: 30 Minutes • **start to finish:** 1 Hour 30 Minutes • **10 servings**

DRESSING

- ⅓ **cup milk**
- ⅓ **cup mayonnaise**
- 3 **tablespoons sugar**
- 3 **tablespoons white wine vinegar**
- 2 **teaspoons poppy seed**
- ½ **teaspoon salt**
- ½ **teaspoon celery salt**
- ½ **teaspoon dry mustard**

SALAD

- 1 **package (16 oz) gemelli pasta**
- 2 **cups diced cooked chicken**
- 1 **cup dried cherries**
- ½ **cup sliced celery**
- ½ **cup slivered almonds, toasted***

1 In small bowl, mix dressing ingredients with whisk until well blended. Cover; refrigerate until ready to use.

2 Cook and drain pasta as directed on package. Rinse with cold water; drain.

3 In large bowl, mix pasta, chicken, cherries and celery. Mix dressing mixture again with whisk; pour over salad and toss gently to coat. Cover; refrigerate 1 to 2 hours, until chilled. Stir in almonds.

*To toast almonds, sprinkle in ungreased skillet. Cook over medium heat 5 to 7 minutes, stirring frequently until nuts begin to brown, then stirring constantly until nuts are light brown.

1 Serving: Calories 410; Total Fat 12g (Saturated Fat 2g; Trans Fat 0g); Cholesterol 25mg; Sodium 290mg; Total Carbohydrate 58g (Dietary Fiber 4g); Protein 18g **Exchanges:** 4 Starch, 1 Lean Meat, 1 Fat **Carbohydrate Choices:** 4

....

Pasta Point

This salad can be made a day ahead; cover and refrigerate. Stir before serving. If needed, add a tablespoon or two of milk to make it creamier.

mediterranean chicken pasta salad

prep time: 25 Minutes • start to finish: 1 Hour 25 Minutes • 6 servings

1 box Betty Crocker Suddenly Salad basil pesto salad mix

⅓ cup water

3 tablespoons olive oil

2 cups cut-up cooked chicken

1 cup cherry or grape tomatoes, halved

1 cup coarsely chopped cucumber

1 cup crumbled feta cheese

1 can (2.25 oz) sliced ripe olives, drained

1 Fill 3-quart saucepan two-thirds full of water; heat to boiling. Empty pasta mix (from Suddenly Salad box) into boiling water. Gently boil uncovered 12 minutes, stirring occasionally.

2 Meanwhile, in large bowl, stir together seasoning mix (from Suddenly Salad box), water and oil. Add chicken; let stand while pasta is cooking. Drain pasta; rinse with cold water. Shake to drain well.

3 Stir drained pasta and remaining ingredients into chicken mixture. Refrigerate at least 1 hour before serving. Cover and refrigerate any remaining salad.

1 Serving: Calories 330; Total Fat 16g (Saturated Fat 5g; Trans Fat 0g); Cholesterol 55mg; Sodium 830mg; Total Carbohydrate 26g (Dietary Fiber 2g); Protein 21g **Exchanges:** 1½ Other Carbohydrate, 3 Lean Meat, 1½ Fat **Carbohydrate Choices:** 2

Pasta Point

Make this salad the day before serving. A delicious dinner will be waiting for you in the fridge the next day.

grilled caesar pasta salad

prep time: 35 Minutes • **start to finish:** 35 Minutes • 4 servings

1 box Betty Crocker Suddenly Salad Caesar salad mix

3 tablespoons olive oil

2 tablespoons lemon juice

1 lb uncooked boneless chicken tenders (not breaded)

1 tablespoon Dijon mustard

2 heads baby romaine lettuce, halved lengthwise

Olive oil for drizzling

Croutons, if desired

Shaved Parmesan cheese, if desired

1 Fill 3-quart saucepan two-thirds full of water; heat to boiling. Empty pasta mix (from Suddenly Salad box) into boiling water. Gently boil uncovered 12 minutes, stirring occasionally. Drain pasta. Rinse with cold water. Shake to drain well.

2 In large bowl, mix seasoning and crouton blend (from Suddenly Salad box), 3 tablespoons olive oil and the lemon juice. Stir in cooked pasta. Cover; refrigerate until ready to serve. In small bowl, coat chicken tenders with mustard; set aside.

3 Heat gas or charcoal grill. Place chicken tenders on grill over medium-high heat. Cover grill; cook chicken tenders about 8 minutes, turning after 4 minutes, until chicken is no longer pink in center. Drizzle lettuce with olive oil. Place lettuce on grill, cut side down. Cook 1 to 2 minutes or just until light grill marks appear.

4 To serve, place pasta mixture on large serving platter. Top with chicken tenders. Arrange lettuce around edges of platter; top with croutons and cheese.

1 Serving: Calories 440; Total Fat 13g (Saturated Fat 1.5g; Trans Fat 0g); Cholesterol 50mg; Sodium 870mg; Total Carbohydrate 48g (Dietary Fiber 7g); Protein 34g **Exchanges:** 2 Starch, 3 Vegetable, 3 Lean Meat, ½ Fat **Carbohydrate Choices:** 3

Improvise
Lightly grilled baby lettuce adds a twist to this flavorful favorite.

chicken pasta salad with poppy seed dressing

prep time: 25 Minutes • **start to finish:** 25 Minutes • 4 servings

1½ **cups uncooked gemelli pasta (6 oz)**

1½ **cups cubed smoked chicken (from deli) (8 oz)**

¾ **cup halved seedless red grapes**

½ **cup thinly sliced celery**

½ **cup refrigerated poppy seed dressing**

1 Cook and drain pasta as directed on package. Rinse with cold water; drain.

2 In large bowl, gently mix cooled cooked pasta, chicken, grapes and celery. Pour dressing over salad; toss to coat well. Serve immediately.

1 Serving: Calories 390; Total Fat 16g (Saturated Fat 2g; Trans Fat 0g); Cholesterol 40mg; Sodium 1170mg; Total Carbohydrate 49g (Dietary Fiber 3g); Protein 16g **Exchanges:** 2 Starch, 1 Other Carbohydrate, 1½ Lean Meat, 2 Fat **Carbohydrate Choices:** 3

Improvise

Add ⅓ cup toasted slivered almonds or cashews to this recipe, if desired. Use Bibb or leaf lettuce to line the bowl. To toast almonds, sprinkle in ungreased skillet. Cook over medium heat 5 to 7 minutes, stirring frequently until nuts begin to brown, then stirring constantly until nuts are light brown.

Three-Ingredient Pasta Sauces

Start with your favorite hot cooked plain or filled pasta and one of these easy flavor-packed sauces. Top with grated, shredded or shaved Asiago or Parmesan cheese. You might also like to offer freshly ground black pepper and crushed red pepper flakes as final garnishes.

Artichoke, Olive and Sun-Dried Tomato Sauce — Heat one 14-ounce can undrained marinated artichoke hearts, coarsely chopped, ¼ cup sliced sun-dried tomatoes in oil and 2 tablespoons chopped, pitted kalamata olives; toss with pasta.

Bacon-Alfredo Sauce — Heat 10 ounces refrigerated Alfredo sauce with 2 slices crisply cooked crumbled bacon and ¼ cup chopped fresh Italian parsley; toss with pasta.

Cheesy Meatball Sauce — Heat one 14-ounce jar double-Cheddar or roasted garlic pasta sauce, 8 ounces hot cooked Italian meatballs (cut in half or quarters) and 2 tablespoons chopped fresh basil; toss with pasta.

Margherita Pasta Sauce — Heat one 14.5-ounce can undrained diced tomatoes with basil, garlic and oregano, and toss with pasta; gently stir in ¼ cup diced fresh mozzarella.

Pepperoni and Olive Sauce — Heat 1 cup tomato pasta sauce or pizza sauce with 4 cups chopped pepperoni and 2 tablespoons sliced ripe olives; toss with or serve over pasta.

Shrimp Marinara Sauce — Heat 10 ounces refrigerated marinara sauce with 8 ounces cooked medium shrimp, 2 tablespoons chopped fresh basil and crushed red pepper flakes, if desired; toss with or serve over pasta.

Margherita Pasta Sauce

Cheesy Meatball Sauce

Shrimp Marinara Sauce

Artichoke, Olive and Sun-Dried
Tomato Sauce

Pepperoni and Olive
Sauce

Bacon-Alfredo Sauce

bacon and basil pasta salad

prep time: 25 Minutes • **start to finish:** 2 Hours 25 Minutes • **22 servings**

1 package (16 oz) uncooked penne pasta

8 oz sliced bacon

1 pint grape tomatoes, halved

2 medium red or green bell peppers or 1 of each, chopped (2 cups)

4 medium green onions, sliced (¼ cup)

⅓ cup red wine vinegar

1 tablespoon Dijon mustard

½ cup olive oil

½ cup chopped fresh basil leaves

1 teaspoon salt

½ teaspoon freshly ground pepper

1 Cook and drain pasta as directed on package. Rinse with cold water; drain.

2 Meanwhile, in 10-inch nonstick skillet, cook bacon over medium heat 5 to 8 minutes until crisp; drain on paper towels. Crumble bacon; refrigerate until serving time.

3 In large bowl, mix pasta, tomatoes, bell peppers and onions.

4 In small bowl, beat vinegar and mustard with whisk. Add oil; beat with whisk until blended. Stir in basil, salt and pepper. Pour over pasta mixture and toss to combine. Cover; refrigerate 2 hours or until chilled.

5 Just before serving, sprinkle bacon over salad and toss to combine.

1 Serving: Calories 160; Total Fat 7g (Saturated Fat 1g; Trans Fat 0g); Cholesterol 0mg; Sodium 270mg; Total Carbohydrate 19g (Dietary Fiber 1g); Protein 4g **Exchanges:** 1 Starch, ½ Vegetable, 1½ Fat **Carbohydrate Choices:** 1

Pasta Points

Grape tomatoes are the smaller version of cherry tomatoes, and they are just about bite-size. Cherry tomatoes, cut in half or into quarters, can be used instead of grape tomatoes in this salad.

Experiment with the bacon. Try peppered bacon or applewood-smoked bacon for a slight flavor variation. If using peppered bacon, taste the salad before seasoning to taste with pepper.

blt pasta salad

prep time: 30 Minutes • **start to finish:** 30 Minutes • 4 servings

DRESSING

- ½ **cup sour cream**
- ¼ **cup mayonnaise**
- 1 **tablespoon white wine vinegar**
- ½ **teaspoon salt**
- ¼ **teaspoon cracked black pepper**

SALAD

- 2 **cups uncooked rotini pasta (6 oz)**
- 1 **package (12 oz) bacon, cut into ½-inch pieces**
- 3 **cups chopped tomatoes (2 to 3 large)**
- 4 **cups lightly packed torn leaf lettuce**

1 In small bowl, stir dressing ingredients until blended.

2 Cook and drain pasta as directed on package. Rinse with cold water; drain.

3 Meanwhile, in 12-inch nonstick skillet, cook bacon over medium heat 5 to 8 minutes, stirring often, until crisp; drain on paper towels. Set aside ¼ cup bacon for garnish.

4 In large bowl, stir tomatoes, dressing and remaining bacon. Stir in pasta. Place lettuce in large shallow bowl. Spoon salad over lettuce; sprinkle with reserved bacon.

1 Serving: Calories 560; Total Fat 28g (Saturated Fat 9g; Trans Fat 0g); Cholesterol 45mg; Sodium 1180mg; Total Carbohydrate 56g (Dietary Fiber 5g); Protein 20g **Exchanges:** 2½ Starch, ½ Other Carbohydrate, 1½ Vegetable, 1½ High-Fat Meat, 3 Fat **Carbohydrate Choices:** 4

Pasta Points

The dressing can be made up to 1 day ahead; cover and refrigerate. Assemble salad just before serving.

Look for juicy ripe tomatoes for this recipe, and store them at room temperature to maintain their flavor. Reserve any leftover tomato juice and seeds from cutting the tomatoes, and add them to the dressing for additional flavor.

tuscan pasta salad

prep time: 25 Minutes • **start to finish:** 2 Hours 25 Minutes • **8 servings**

3 cups uncooked bow-tie (farfalle) pasta (8 oz)

4 oz hard salami, cut into thin strips (about 1x¼ inch)

1 medium red bell pepper, chopped (1 cup)

½ medium red onion, chopped (about 1 cup)

⅓ cup red wine vinegar

2 cloves garlic, finely chopped

¼ teaspoon pepper

½ cup olive oil

1 package (9 oz) romaine salad mix or 6 cups torn romaine

½ cup shredded Parmesan cheese

1 Cook and drain pasta as directed on package. Rinse with cold water; drain.

2 In large bowl, mix pasta, salami, bell pepper and onion.

3 In small bowl, mix vinegar, garlic and pepper. Add oil; beat with whisk until blended. Pour over pasta mixture and toss to combine. Cover; refrigerate 2 hours or until chilled.

4 Just before serving, add romaine and toss to combine. Sprinkle with cheese.

1 Serving: Calories 340; Total Fat 20g (Saturated Fat 4.5g; Trans Fat 0g); Cholesterol 20mg; Sodium 510mg; Total Carbohydrate 28g (Dietary Fiber 2g); Protein 11g **Exchanges:** 1 Starch, ½ Other Carbohydrate, ½ Vegetable, ½ Lean Meat, ½ High-Fat Meat, 3 Fat **Carbohydrate Choices:** 2

Improvise

If you're a pepperoni fan, substitute it for the salami.

Pasta Point

This salad can be prepared the day before—except don't add the romaine until right before serving time so it doesn't wilt.

dijon ham and pasta salad

prep time: 20 Minutes • **start to finish:** 20 Minutes • **4 servings**

1 box Betty Crocker Suddenly Salad classic pasta salad mix

3 tablespoons cold water

2 tablespoons vegetable oil

2 tablespoons Dijon mustard

1 cup cubed fully cooked ham

1 can (14 oz) artichoke hearts, drained, cut into quarters

••••••••••••••••••••••••••••••••••

Improvise

Stir in bagged broccoli florets or shredded carrots for a veggie-packed salad.

1 Fill 3-quart saucepan two-thirds full of water; heat to boiling. Empty pasta mix (from Suddenly Salad box) into boiling water. Gently boil uncovered 12 minutes, stirring occasionally.

2 Meanwhile, in large bowl, stir together seasoning mix (from Suddenly Salad box), water, oil and mustard.

3 Drain pasta; rinse with cold water. Shake to drain well. Stir pasta, ham and artichokes into dressing mixture. Serve immediately, or cover and refrigerate up to 2 hours before serving.

1 Serving: Calories 360; Total Fat 12g (Saturated Fat 2g; Trans Fat 0g); Cholesterol 20mg; Sodium 1820mg; Total Carbohydrate 47g (Dietary Fiber 6g); Protein 17g **Exchanges:** 3 Starch, 1 Very Lean Meat, 2 Fat **Carbohydrate Choices:** 3

prosciutto and olive pasta salad

prep time: 20 Minutes • **start to finish:** 20 Minutes • **4 servings**

1¾ cups uncooked multigrain penne pasta

2 cups fresh baby spinach leaves

8 jalapeño-stuffed green olives, sliced

2 oz thinly sliced prosciutto, chopped

2 tablespoons chopped fresh oregano leaves

1 tablespoon olive oil

⅓ cup crumbled reduced-fat feta cheese

1 Cook pasta as directed on package, omitting salt and oil; drain. Rinse with cold water; drain well.

2 In large bowl, stir together spinach, olives, prosciutto, oregano and oil. Add pasta and cheese; toss well.

1 Serving: Calories 290; Total Fat 8g (Saturated Fat 2.5g; Trans Fat 0g); Cholesterol 15mg; Sodium 510mg; Total Carbohydrate 39g (Dietary Fiber 5g); Protein 14g **Exchanges:** 2 Starch, ½ Other Carbohydrate, ½ Vegetable, ½ Very Lean Meat, ½ Lean Meat, 1 Fat **Carbohydrate Choices:** 2½

Pasta Pairing

Sweet and juicy cantaloupe makes a delicious accompaniment to this tangy dish.

sesame singapore shrimp salad

prep time: 25 Minutes • **start to finish:** 25 Minutes • **4 servings**

1 box Betty Crocker™ Suddenly Salad™ classic pasta salad mix

⅔ cup Asian toasted sesame salad dressing

½ teaspoon crushed red pepper flakes

2 cups angel hair or regular coleslaw mix

1½ cups coarsely chopped cooked peeled shrimp

¼ cup chopped dry-roasted peanuts

¼ cup finely chopped basil leaves

1 mango, seed removed, peeled and cut into ½-inch cubes (1 cup)

1 medium green onion, chopped (1 tablespoon)

Black sesame seed

1 Fill 3-quart saucepan two-thirds full of water; heat to boiling. Empty pasta mix (from Suddenly Salad box) into boiling water. Gently boil uncovered 12 minutes, stirring occasionally.

2 Meanwhile, in large bowl, stir together seasoning mix (from Suddenly Salad box), salad dressing and pepper flakes. Add coleslaw, shrimp, peanuts, basil leaves, mango and green onion; toss gently to coat.

3 Drain pasta; rinse with cold water. Shake to drain well. Stir pasta into salad mixture. Sprinkle with sesame seed. Serve immediately, or cover and refrigerate until serving.

1 Serving: Calories 550; Total Fat 20g (Saturated Fat 3g; Trans Fat 0g); Cholesterol 180mg; Sodium 1580mg; Total Carbohydrate 64g (Dietary Fiber 3g); Protein 28g
Exchanges: 2 Starch, ½ Fruit, 1½ Other Carbohydrate, ½ Vegetable, 3 Lean Meat, 2 Fat **Carbohydrate Choices:** 4

Pasta Point

Buy peeled and precut mango in the produce section of your supermarket. You may need to chop more finely.

orzo and tuna salad

prep time: 25 Minutes • **start to finish:** 25 Minutes • 4 servings

1 cup uncooked orzo or rosamarina pasta (6 oz)

1 package (3 oz) cream cheese, softened

1½ cups diced cucumber (about 1 medium)

3 tablespoons cider vinegar

2 medium stalks celery, thinly sliced (1 cup)

1 tablespoon olive or vegetable oil

2 cans (5 oz each) albacore tuna in water, drained

2 tablespoons chopped fresh dill weed

½ teaspoon salt

¼ teaspoon pepper

1 Cook and drain pasta as directed on package. Rinse with cold water; drain.

2 Meanwhile, in food processor, place cream cheese, 1 cup of the cucumber, the vinegar, celery and oil. Cover; process until smooth.

3 In large bowl, stir cooked pasta, cream cheese mixture, remaining ½ cup cucumber and remaining ingredients until well mixed.

1 Serving: Calories 380; Total Fat 13g (Saturated Fat 6g; Trans Fat 0g); Cholesterol 45mg; Sodium 920mg; Total Carbohydrate 40g (Dietary Fiber 3g); Protein 27g **Exchanges:** 1½ Starch, ½ Low-Fat Milk, 2 Vegetable, 2 Lean Meat, 1 Fat **Carbohydrate Choices:** 2½

seaside blt pasta salad

prep time: 20 Minutes • start to finish: 1 Hour 20 Minutes • 6 servings

1 box Betty Crocker
Suddenly Salad ranch &
bacon salad mix

¾ cup mayonnaise

2 tablespoons milk

2 tablespoons lemon juice

3 cans (6 oz each) lump
crabmeat, drained, rinsed

¼ cup thinly sliced green
onions (4 medium)

4 slices bacon, crisply
cooked, crumbled (¼ cup)

2 cups thinly sliced
iceberg lettuce

2 medium tomatoes,
chopped, drained (1½ cups)

1 Fill 3-quart saucepan two-thirds full of water; heat to boiling. Empty pasta mix (from Suddenly Salad box) into boiling water. Gently boil uncovered 12 minutes, stirring occasionally.

2 Meanwhile, in large bowl, stir together seasoning mix (from Suddenly Salad box), mayonnaise, milk and lemon juice. Stir in crabmeat, onions and bacon.

3 Drain pasta; rinse with cold water. Shake to drain well. Stir pasta into salad mixture. Cover; refrigerate 1 hour to chill. Just before serving, gently toss with lettuce and tomatoes to coat.

1 Serving: Calories 490; Total Fat 26g (Saturated Fat 4g; Trans Fat 0g); Cholesterol 100mg; Sodium 850mg; Total Carbohydrate 38g (Dietary Fiber 2g); Protein 25g **Exchanges:** 2 Starch, ½ Other Carbohydrate, 3 Lean Meat, 3 Fat **Carbohydrate Choices:** 2½

Improvise

Slim down this salad by using fat-free mayo and turkey bacon.

sesame noodle salad

prep time: 25 Minutes • start to finish: 25 Minutes • 12 servings

SESAME DRESSING

- 3 tablespoons vegetable oil
- 3 tablespoons soy sauce
- 1 tablespoon balsamic or rice vinegar
- 1 tablespoon dark sesame oil
- 4½ teaspoons sugar
- 1½ teaspoons grated gingerroot
- ½ teaspoon garlic powder
- ⅛ teaspoon ground red pepper (cayenne)

SALAD

- 8 oz uncooked soba (buckwheat) noodles or angel hair (capellini) pasta
- 2 medium carrots, shredded (1 cup)
- 1 small cucumber, cut lengthwise in half, then cut crosswise into thin slices
- 2 medium green onions, thinly sliced (2 tablespoons)
- 1 tablespoon sesame seed, toasted*

1 In small bowl, stir dressing ingredients until well mixed; set aside.

2 In 4-quart Dutch oven or saucepan, heat 2 quarts water to boiling. Cook noodles in boiling water 6 to 8 minutes or until tender (if using angel hair pasta, cook as directed on package); drain. Rinse with cold water; drain.

3 In large bowl, toss noodles, dressing and remaining salad ingredients. Cover; refrigerate until serving.

*To toast sesame seed, sprinkle in ungreased skillet. Cook over medium-low heat 5 to 7 minutes, stirring frequently until browning begins, then stirring constantly until golden brown.

1 Serving: Calories 120; Total Fat 5g (Saturated Fat 1g; Trans Fat 0g); Cholesterol 0mg; Sodium 230mg; Total Carbohydrate 16g (Dietary Fiber 2g); Protein 3g **Exchanges:** 1 Starch, 1 Fat **Carbohydrate Choices:** 1

Pasta Point

Light-colored sesame oil has a delicate, nutty flavor, while dark sesame oil has a stronger, robust flavor.

layered pasta caprese salad

prep time: 35 Minutes • start to finish: 1 Hour • 10 servings

3 tablespoons salt

1 lb uncooked orecchiette (tiny disk) pasta

3 cups ½-inch marinated bocconcini, drained and marinating liquid reserved

Olive oil, if necessary

1 lb red heirloom tomatoes, sliced

1 lb yellow or orange heirloom tomatoes, sliced

½ teaspoon salt

½ cup balsamic vinegar

3 cups basil leaves

1 In large stockpot, heat 3 quarts water to boiling. Add 3 tablespoons salt; return to boiling. Add pasta; cook as directed on package. Drain and cool slightly, then toss with 1 cup of the reserved marinating liquid from the bocconcini (if there is less than 1 cup marinating liquid, add enough olive oil to liquid to make 1 cup). Refrigerate to cool completely.

2 Place tomatoes on ungreased baking pan with sides, divided by color; sprinkle with ½ teaspoon salt. Set aside 15 minutes, then pat dry with paper towels.

3 In 1-quart saucepan, heat balsamic vinegar to a simmer over medium heat. Simmer 10 to 15 minutes or until reduced by half. Set aside to cool.

4 In 3½-quart trifle dish or large glass bowl, layer as follows: Gently layer half of the pasta, then one-third of the basil leaves, then one layer of all the red tomatoes. Top the tomatoes with the bocconcini, then the rest of the pasta, another one-third of the basil, then the yellow tomatoes. Drizzle with the cooled balsamic vinegar.

5 Shred remaining basil, and sprinkle on top.

1 Serving: Calories 660 (Calories from Fat 260); Total Fat 29g (Saturated Fat 17g, Trans Fat 0.5g); Cholesterol 95mg; Sodium 880mg; Potassium 520mg; Total Carbohydrate 66g (Dietary Fiber 5g); Protein 35g **Exchanges:** 2 Starch, 2½ Milk, 1 Vegetable, 1 High-Fat Meat 2 Starch, 1½ Vegetable, 1 Fat **Carbohydrate Choices:** 4½

• •

Pasta Point

Orecchiette, or "little ears" in Italian, is a lovely small shaped pasta. If you have trouble finding it, you can use your favorite shaped pasta in its place.

hearty soybean and cheddar pasta salad

prep time: 35 Minutes • **start to finish:** 1 Hour 35 Minutes • **4 servings**

SALAD

- 1 cup uncooked penne pasta (3 oz)
- 1 bag (12 oz) frozen shelled edamame (green soybeans)
- 1 large tomato, coarsely chopped (1 cup)
- 1 small yellow bell pepper, coarsely chopped (½ cup)
- ½ medium cucumber, coarsely chopped (½ cup)
- 6 oz Cheddar cheese, cut into ½-inch cubes (1½ cups)

DRESSING

- ⅓ cup vegetable oil
- ¼ cup red wine vinegar
- 1 teaspoon Italian seasoning
- ½ teaspoon salt
- ¼ teaspoon pepper
- ¼ teaspoon garlic powder

1 Cook pasta and soybeans separately as directed on each package. Rinse with cold water; drain.

2 In large bowl, toss pasta, soybeans, tomato, bell pepper, cucumber and cheese. In small bowl, beat dressing ingredients with whisk until well mixed. Pour over salad; toss.

3 Cover; refrigerate at least 1 hour to blend flavors. Stir before serving.

1 Serving: Calories 710; Total Fat 45g (Saturated Fat 13g; Trans Fat 0g); Cholesterol 45mg; Sodium 780mg; Total Carbohydrate 39g (Dietary Fiber 11g); Protein 37g **Exchanges:** 2 Starch, 3 High-Fat Meat, 2½ Fat **Carbohydrate Choices:** 2½

Pasta Point

Edamame is the Japanese name for fresh green soybeans—tasty little bright green gems that cook quickly and are high in protein.

texas-style pasta salad

prep time: 30 Minutes • **start to finish:** 30 Minutes • 20 servings

1 package (16 oz) penne pasta

1 can (4 oz) whole green chiles, drained, chopped

1 medium red bell pepper, chopped (1 cup)

8 oz Cheddar cheese, cut into ½-inch cubes (1¾ cups)

3 medium green onions, chopped (3 tablespoons)

½ cup chopped fresh cilantro

1 cup medium taco sauce

¼ cup vegetable oil

2 tablespoons lime juice

½ to 1 teaspoon ground cumin

1 cup nacho-flavored tortilla chips, coarsely crushed

1 Cook and drain pasta as directed on package. Rinse with cold water; drain.

2 In large bowl, mix pasta, chiles, bell pepper, cheese, onions and cilantro.

3 In small bowl, mix taco sauce, oil, lime juice and cumin. Pour over pasta mixture and toss gently to combine. Top with crushed tortilla chips. Serve immediately.

1 Serving: Calories 200; Total Fat 8g (Saturated Fat 3g; Trans Fat 0g); Cholesterol 10mg; Sodium 280mg; Total Carbohydrate 24g (Dietary Fiber 1g); Protein 7g **Exchanges:** 1½ Starch, ½ High-Fat Meat, ½ Fat **Carbohydrate Choices:** 1½

....

Improvise

Roasted red bell peppers from a jar, drained and chopped, can be substituted for the fresh bell pepper.

Try pepper Jack cheese instead of Cheddar.

speedway pasta salad

prep: 25 Minutes • total: 2 Hours 25 Minutes • 12 servings

1 package (16 oz) wagon wheel pasta or rotini pasta

1 can (8 oz) tomato sauce

1 cup reduced-fat Italian dressing

1 tablespoon chopped fresh or 1 teaspoon dried basil leaves

1 tablespoon fresh or 1 teaspoon dried oregano leaves

1 cup sliced fresh mushrooms

5 plum (Roma) tomatoes, coarsely chopped (1½ cups)

1 large peeled or unpeeled cucumber, coarsely chopped (1½ cups)

1 medium red onion, chopped (½ cup)

1 can (2.25 oz) sliced ripe olives, drained

1 Cook and drain pasta as directed on package. Rinse with cold water; drain.

2 In large bowl, mix tomato sauce, dressing, basil and oregano. Add remaining ingredients; toss.

3 Cover and refrigerate at least 2 hours or until chilled, but no longer than 48 hours.

1 Serving: Calories 220; Total Fat 4.5g (Saturated Fat 0.5g; Trans Fat 0g); Cholesterol 0mg; Sodium 580mg; Total Carbohydrate 39g (Dietary Fiber 3g); Protein 7g **Exchanges:** 2 Starch, ½ Other Carbohydrate, ½ Vegetable, ½ Fat **Carbohydrate Choices:** 2½

Improvise

To make this a main dish, stir in leftover cooked meat or a can of drained, rinsed beans.

Pasta Point

Plum (Roma) tomatoes are a perfect choice for pasta salads. Their meaty texture stands up to tossing without a lot of juice to make the salad soggy.

gazpacho pasta salad

prep time: 35 Minutes • **start to finish:** 35 Minutes • **14 servings**

SALAD

1   package (16 oz) bow-tie (farfalle) pasta

2   large tomatoes, seeded, coarsely chopped (2 cups)

1   large cucumber, coarsely chopped (1½ cups)

1   small red bell pepper, coarsely chopped (½ cup)

1   small yellow bell pepper, coarsely chopped (½ cup)

8   medium green onions, sliced (½ cup)

1   green Anaheim chile, seeded, chopped

1   can (2.25 oz) sliced ripe olives, drained

½   cup finely chopped fresh cilantro

TOMATO-LIME VINAIGRETTE

½   cup tomato juice

¼   cup olive or vegetable oil

¼   cup lime juice

½   teaspoon salt

¼   teaspoon pepper

2   cloves garlic, finely chopped

1 Cook and drain pasta as directed on package. Rinse with cold water; drain.

2 In large bowl, mix pasta and remaining salad ingredients.

3 In small bowl, mix vinaigrette ingredients until well blended. Pour over salad; toss to mix.

1 Serving: Calories 200; Total Fat 5g (Saturated Fat 1g; Trans Fat 0g); Cholesterol 0mg; Sodium 260mg; Total Carbohydrate 32g (Dietary Fiber 3g); Protein 6g **Exchanges:** 2 Starch, ½ Vegetable, 1 Fat **Carbohydrate Choices:** 2

Pasta Point

Gazpacho, a cold soup, is a hot-weather favorite that originated in southern Spain. It is traditionally a mixture of pureed fresh tomatoes, bell peppers, onions, cucumbers, garlic, olive oil and lemon juice.

sunny broccoli pasta salad

prep time: 25 Minutes • **start to finish:** 25 Minutes • 8 servings

1 box Betty Crocker Suddenly Salad ranch & bacon salad mix

1 cup mayonnaise

2 tablespoons sugar

2 tablespoons cider vinegar

4 cups small fresh broccoli florets

¼ cup chopped red onion

½ cup raisins

½ cup sunflower nuts

Improvise

For a leaner summer salad, use reduced-fat or fat-free mayonnaise.

Pasta Point

Purchase precut broccoli in bags from the produce section.

1 Fill 3-quart saucepan two-thirds full of water; heat to boiling. Empty pasta mix (from Suddenly Salad box) into boiling water. Gently boil uncovered 12 minutes, stirring occasionally.

2 Meanwhile, in large bowl, stir together seasoning mix (from Suddenly Salad box), mayonnaise, sugar and vinegar.

3 Drain pasta; rinse with cold water. Shake to drain well. Stir pasta, broccoli, onion, raisins and sunflower nuts into dressing mixture. Serve immediately, or refrigerate up to 24 hours before serving.

1 Serving: Calories 420; Total Fat 27g (Saturated Fat 4g; Trans Fat 0g); Cholesterol 10mg; Sodium 380mg; Total Carbohydrate 35g (Dietary Fiber 3g); Protein 8g **Exchanges:** 1 Starch, 1 Other Carbohydrate, 1 Vegetable, ½ High-Fat Meat, 4½ Fat
Carbohydrate Choices: 2

ranch spinach pasta salad

prep time: 15 Minutes • **start to finish:** 15 Minutes • 6 servings

1 box Betty Crocker Suddenly Salad classic pasta salad mix

½ cup ranch dressing

1 tablespoon lemon juice

2 cups baby spinach leaves or small broccoli florets

¾ cup grape tomatoes, halved

½ cup sliced cucumber, halved

½ cup julienne carrots

2 tablespoons chopped fresh or 1 teaspoon dried basil leaves

1 Fill 3-quart saucepan two-thirds full of water; heat to boiling. Empty pasta mix (from Suddenly Salad box) into boiling water. Gently boil uncovered 12 minutes, stirring occasionally.

2 Meanwhile, in medium bowl, stir contents of seasoning mix (from Suddenly Salad box), dressing and lemon juice until blended.

3 Drain pasta; rinse with cold water. Shake to drain well. Stir pasta and remaining ingredients into dressing mixture. Cover; refrigerate until ready to serve.

1 Serving: Calories 220; Total Fat 10g (Saturated Fat 1g; Trans Fat 0g); Cholesterol 5mg; Sodium 830mg; Total Carbohydrate 28g (Dietary Fiber 2g); Protein 5g **Exchanges:** 1½ Starch, ½ Other Carbohydrate, 2 Fat **Carbohydrate Choices:** 2

....

Improvise

Make it a dinner salad. Just stir in 1½ cups cut up cooked chicken or ham.

fattoush pasta salad

prep time: 30 Minutes • start to finish: 1 Hour 30 Minutes • 10 servings

1 box Betty Crocker Suddenly Salad classic pasta salad mix

⅓ cup olive oil

¼ cup lemon juice

2 teaspoons Greek seasoning

1½ cups coarsely chopped cucumber

1 cup coarsely chopped romaine lettuce

1 cup crumbled feta cheese

1 cup grape tomatoes, halved

½ cup thinly sliced zucchini, slices cut into quarters

⅓ cup thinly sliced radishes

⅓ cup chopped red onion

⅓ cup chopped fresh Italian (flat-leaf) parsley

1 tablespoon finely chopped fresh mint leaves

2 cups garlic-flavored croutons

1 Fill 3-quart saucepan two-thirds full of water; heat to boiling. Empty pasta mix (from Suddenly Salad box) into boiling water. Gently boil uncovered 12 minutes, stirring occasionally.

2 Meanwhile, in large bowl, stir together seasoning mix (from Suddenly Salad box), oil, lemon juice and Greek seasoning.

3 Drain pasta; rinse with cold water. Shake to drain well. Add pasta and remaining ingredients to dressing mixture; toss gently. Cover and refrigerate 1 hour to chill.

1 Serving: Calories 220; Total Fat 12g (Saturated Fat 3g; Trans Fat 0.5g); Cholesterol 10mg; Sodium 790mg; Total Carbohydrate 25g (Dietary Fiber 1g); Protein 5g **Exchanges:** 1½ Starch, 2½ Fat **Carbohydrate Choices:** 1½

Pasta Points

Fattoush is an Eastern Mediterranean salad made from vegetables like cucumber, radishes and tomatoes plus toasted or fried pieces of pita bread. The vegetables are cut into relatively large pieces compared with tabbouleh, where ingredients are finely chopped.

All-purpose Greek seasoning is a ground specialty seasoning blend found where the herbs and spices are located in the grocery store.

layered curry pasta salad

prep time: 30 Minutes • **start to finish:** 30 Minutes • 11 servings

1 box Betty Crocker Suddenly Salad ranch & bacon salad mix

3 cups torn salad greens

2 cups shredded carrots

2 cups frozen sweet peas, cooked, drained

2 medium tomatoes, chopped (1½ cups)

1½ cups mayonnaise

1 teaspoon curry powder

½ cup sliced almonds, toasted*

1 Fill 3-quart saucepan two-thirds full of water; heat to boiling. Empty pasta mix (from Suddenly Salad box) into boiling water. Gently boil uncovered 12 minutes, stirring occasionally.

2 Meanwhile, in 4-quart glass salad bowl or 13x9-inch (3-quart) glass baking dish, layer salad greens, carrots, peas and tomatoes.

3 Drain pasta; rinse with cold water. Shake to drain well.

4 In large bowl, stir together seasoning mix (from Suddenly Salad box), mayonnaise and curry powder; stir in pasta. Spread pasta mixture over vegetables in salad bowl. Just before serving, sprinkle with almonds. Serve immediately, or refrigerate up to 2 hours before serving.

*To toast almonds, sprinkle in ungreased skillet. Cook over medium heat 5 to 7 minutes, stirring frequently until almonds begin to brown, then stirring constantly until they are light brown.

1 Serving: Calories 350; Total Fat 26g (Saturated Fat 4g; Trans Fat 0g); Cholesterol 10mg; Sodium 360mg; Total Carbohydrate 22g (Dietary Fiber 3g); Protein 6g **Exchanges:** 1 Starch, 1 Vegetable, 5 Fat **Carbohydrate Choices:** 1½

• •

Improvise

For a leaner summer salad, use reduced-fat or fat-free mayonnaise.

italian pasta salad

prep time: 30 Minutes • **start to finish:** 1 Hour 30 Minutes • 24 servings

DRESSING

- ¼ cup marinade from the artichoke hearts
- ¼ cup olive oil
- 2 tablespoons red wine vinegar
- 2 tablespoons finely chopped fresh basil
- 1 tablespoon chopped fresh Italian (flat-leaf) parsley
- 2 teaspoons Dijon mustard
- ¼ teaspoon salt
- ½ teaspoon pepper

SALAD

- 1 package (12 oz) rainbow rotini pasta
- 1 jar (12 oz) marinated artichoke hearts, drained, marinade reserved
- 8 oz mozzarella cheese, cut into ½-inch cubes
- 1 English (seedless) cucumber, chopped (about 2 cups)
- 1 pint (2 cups) cherry tomatoes, halved
- 1 cup finely chopped red onion
- 1 cup sliced radishes
- ⅓ cup chopped celery
- ⅓ cup sliced green olives
- ¼ cup sliced green onions

1 In small jar with tight-fitting lid, shake dressing ingredients.

2 Cook pasta as directed on package; drain. Rinse with cold water; drain.

3 In large bowl, stir together remaining salad ingredients with pasta. Pour dressing over top; toss gently to coat. Refrigerate at least 1 hour before serving.

1 Serving: Calories 130; Total Fat 5g (Saturated Fat 1.5g; Trans Fat 0g); Cholesterol 5mg; Sodium 210mg; Total Carbohydrate 16g (Dietary Fiber 2g); Protein 5g **Exchanges:** ½ Starch, 2 Vegetable, 1 Fat **Carbohydrate Choices:** 1

southwest pasta salad

prep time: 30 Minutes • **start to finish:** 30 Minutes • 12 servings

2 boxes Betty Crocker Suddenly Salad classic salad mix

½ cup cold water

⅓ cup olive oil

2 tablespoons cider vinegar

1 tablespoon chopped fresh cilantro leaves

1 to 2 tablespoons red pepper sauce, if desired

½ teaspoon ground cumin

1 can (15 oz) black beans, drained, rinsed

1 can (14.5 oz) diced tomatoes with jalapeño peppers, drained

1 can (11 oz) whole kernel corn with red and green peppers, drained

½ cup sliced ripe olives

½ cup chopped red, yellow or green bell pepper

1 medium avocado, pitted, peeled and cut into ½-inch cubes

8 oz pepper Jack cheese, cut into ½-inch cubes (2 cups)

Lettuce leaves, if desired

1 Fill 3-quart saucepan two-thirds full of water; heat to boiling. Empty pasta mix (from Suddenly Salad box) into boiling water. Gently boil uncovered 12 minutes, stirring occasionally.

2 Meanwhile, in large bowl, mix contents of seasoning pouches (from Suddenly Salad box), cold water, oil, vinegar, cilantro, pepper sauce and cumin.

3 Drain pasta; rinse with cold water. Shake to drain well. Add pasta, beans, tomatoes, corn, olives, bell pepper, avocado and cheese to seasoning mixture; toss gently to coat. Serve immediately on lettuce-lined platter, or cover and refrigerate until serving time.

1 Serving: Calories 340; Total Fat 14g (Saturated Fat 4g; Trans Fat 0g); Cholesterol 15mg; Sodium 920mg; Total Carbohydrate 42g (Dietary Fiber 5g); Protein 11g **Exchanges:** 2½ Starch, ½ Other Carbohydrate, ½ High-Fat Meat, 1½ Fat **Carbohydrate Choices:** 3

Pasta Point

Make this salad up to 24 hours ahead. Give it a stir before serving.

CHAPTER 4

One-Pot Soups

italian chicken noodle soup

prep time: 25 Minutes • **start to finish:** 35 Minutes • 6 servings

1 tablespoon olive or vegetable oil

8 oz boneless skinless chicken breasts, cut into ½-inch pieces

1 medium onion, chopped (½ cup)

1 carton (32 oz) chicken broth (4 cups)

2 cups water

3 medium carrots, sliced (1½ cups)

2 cups fresh broccoli florets

1½ cups uncooked egg noodles (3 oz)

1 teaspoon dried basil leaves

½ teaspoon garlic-pepper blend

¼ cup shredded Parmesan cheese

1 In 4-quart Dutch oven or saucepan, heat oil over medium heat. Cook chicken in oil 4 to 6 minutes, stirring occasionally, until no longer pink in center. Add onion. Cook 2 to 3 minutes longer, stirring occasionally, until onion is tender.

2 Stir in broth, water and carrots. Heat to boiling over medium heat. Cook 5 minutes. Stir in broccoli, noodles, basil and garlic-pepper blend. Heat to boiling; reduce heat. Simmer uncovered 8 to 10 minutes, stirring occasionally, until vegetables and noodles are tender.

3 Top individual servings with cheese and serve.

1 Serving: Calories 170; Total Fat 6g (Saturated Fat 2g; Trans Fat 0g); Cholesterol 35mg; Sodium 710mg; Total Carbohydrate 13g (Dietary Fiber 2g); Protein 15g **Exchanges:** 1 Starch, 1½ Very Lean Meat, 1 Fat **Carbohydrate Choices:** 1

Improvise

You can substitute chicken thighs for part or all of the chicken breasts. And you can use frozen carrots and broccoli instead of fresh, if you like.

tortellini soup

prep time: 40 Minutes • **start to finish:** 1 Hour • **10 servings**

3 tablespoons butter

2 cloves garlic,
  finely chopped

2 medium stalks celery,
  chopped (1 cup)

1 medium carrot, chopped
  (½ cup)

1 small onion, chopped
  (⅓ cup)

2 cartons (32 oz each)
  chicken broth (8 cups)

4 cups water

2 packages (7 oz each) dried
  cheese-filled tortellini

2 tablespoons chopped
  fresh parsley

½ teaspoon pepper

1 teaspoon freshly grated
  whole nutmeg

  Grated Parmesan cheese

1 Melt butter in 6-quart Dutch oven or saucepan over medium-low heat. Cook garlic, celery, carrot and onion in butter, covered, 10 minutes, stirring occasionally.

2 Stir in broth and water. Heat to boiling; reduce heat. Stir in tortellini. Cover and simmer about 20 minutes, stirring occasionally, until tortellini are tender.

3 Stir in parsley, pepper and nutmeg. Cover and simmer 10 minutes. Top each serving with cheese.

1 Serving: Calories 210; Total Fat 9g (Saturated Fat 3.5g, Trans Fat 0g); Cholesterol 40mg; Sodium 1030mg; Total Carbohydrate 27g (Dietary Fiber 2g); Protein 6g **Exchanges:** 2 Starch, 1½ Fat **Carbohydrate Choices:** 2

Improvise
Try using half spinach and half plain tortellini for an interesting visual presentation.

chicken and broccoli tortellini soup

prep time: 25 Minutes • **start to finish:** 25 Minutes • 4 servings

1 tablespoon olive or vegetable oil

1 small onion, chopped (⅓ cup)

1¾ cups chicken broth (from 32-oz carton)

½ cup water

½ teaspoon Italian seasoning

1 bag (12 oz) frozen broccoli and cheese sauce

1 package (9 oz) refrigerated cheese-filled tortellini

1 cup cubed cooked chicken

1 large plum (Roma) tomato, chopped (½ cup)

¼ cup shredded Parmesan cheese

1 In 2-quart saucepan, heat oil over medium-high heat. Add onion; cook about 2 minutes, stirring frequently, until crisp-tender.

2 Stir in broth, water, Italian seasoning, frozen broccoli and cheese sauce and tortellini. Heat to boiling, stirring occasionally and breaking up broccoli.

3 Stir in chicken. Cook about 4 minutes longer, stirring occasionally, until tortellini is tender. Stir in tomato. Top each serving with 1 tablespoon cheese.

1 Serving: Calories 370; Total Fat 14g (Saturated Fat 5g; Trans Fat 0g); Cholesterol 60mg; Sodium 1150mg; Total Carbohydrate 37g (Dietary Fiber 3g); Protein 25g **Exchanges:** 1½ Starch, ½ Other Carbohydrate, 1 Vegetable, 2½ Medium-Fat Meat **Carbohydrate Choices:** 2½

Pasta Pairing

Serve this delicious, hearty soup with warm slices of French bread.

creamy chicken noodle soup with pesto drizzle

prep time: 35 Minutes • **start to finish:** 35 Minutes • 6 servings

2 tablespoons butter

2 medium carrots, sliced (1 cup)

2 medium stalks celery, sliced (1 cup)

1 medium onion, chopped (½ cup)

1 carton (32 oz) reduced-sodium chicken broth (4 cups)

2½ cups milk

1 box Tuna Helper™ creamy broccoli

2 cups cut-up cooked chicken

1 dried bay leaf

2 tablespoons basil pesto

1 In 5-quart Dutch oven or saucepan, melt butter over medium heat. Cook carrots, celery and onion in butter about 5 minutes, stirring frequently, until carrots are crisp-tender.

2 Stir in broth, milk, uncooked pasta and sauce mix (from Tuna Helper box), chicken and bay leaf. Heat to boiling; reduce heat. Simmer uncovered 12 to 15 minutes, stirring occasionally, until pasta and vegetables are tender.

3 Remove bay leaf; ladle soup into bowls. Place pesto in small resealable food-storage plastic bag; seal bag. Cut off tiny corner of bag; drizzle pesto over soup.

1 Serving: Calories 280; Total Fat 15g (Saturated Fat 6g; Trans Fat 0g); Cholesterol 60mg; Sodium 660mg; Total Carbohydrate 16g (Dietary Fiber 1g); Protein 19g **Exchanges:** 1 Starch, 2½ Lean Meat, 1 Fat **Carbohydrate Choices:** 1

chicken, squash and pasta soup

prep time: 40 Minutes • **start to finish:** 40 Minutes • **6 servings**

1 tablespoon olive or vegetable oil

2 medium stalks celery, coarsely chopped (1 cup)

1 medium onion, coarsely chopped (½ cup)

1 teaspoon dried sage leaves

6 cups chicken broth (from two 32-oz cartons)

2½ cups chopped deli rotisserie chicken (from 2-lb chicken)

1½ cups uncooked tricolor rotini pasta (about 5 oz)

1½ cups cubes (¾ inch) peeled butternut squash

¼ teaspoon salt

⅛ teaspoon pepper

1 In 4½- to 5-quart Dutch oven or saucepan, heat oil over medium-high heat. Add celery, onion and sage; cook 5 to 6 minutes, stirring frequently, until onion is softened.

2 Stir in remaining ingredients. Heat to boiling. Reduce heat to medium; cover and cook 12 to 15 minutes, stirring occasionally, until pasta and squash are tender.

1 Serving: Calories 270; Total Fat 8g (Saturated Fat 2g; Trans Fat 0g); Cholesterol 50mg; Sodium 1420mg; Total Carbohydrate 24g (Dietary Fiber 2g); Protein 25g **Exchanges:** 1 Starch, 1 Vegetable, 3 Lean Meat **Carbohydrate Choices:** 1½

Pasta Point

This recipe calls for the peanut-shaped butternut squash, which, for convenience, is sometimes available precut for cooking.

weeknight chicken noodle soup

prep time: 30 Minutes • **start to finish:** 30 Minutes • **4 servings**

2 cups cut-up rotisserie or other cooked chicken

2 medium stalks celery, chopped (1 cup)

2 medium carrots, sliced (1 cup)

1 medium onion, chopped (½ cup)

1 tablespoon chopped fresh parsley or 1 teaspoon parsley flakes

1 teaspoon dried thyme leaves

¼ teaspoon pepper

2 cloves garlic, finely chopped

7 cups chicken broth (from two 32-oz cartons)

1 cup uncooked wide egg noodles (2 oz)

1 In 3-quart saucepan, heat all ingredients except noodles to boiling. Stir in noodles. Heat to boiling; reduce heat.

2 Simmer uncovered 8 to 10 minutes, stirring occasionally, until noodles and vegetables are tender.

1 Serving: Calories 260; Total Fat 8g (Saturated Fat 2g; Trans Fat 0g); Cholesterol 70mg; Sodium 2070mg; Total Carbohydrate 17g (Dietary Fiber 2g); Protein 30g **Exchanges:** 1 Starch, 4 Very Lean Meat, 1 Fat **Carbohydrate Choices:** 1

Improvise

You can make this recipe a bit quicker by substituting ¼ to ½ teaspoon garlic powder for the chopped fresh garlic.

slow-cooker italian chicken-pasta soup

prep time: 10 Minutes • **start to finish:** 8 Hours 10 Minutes • 6 servings

1¼ lb boneless skinless chicken thighs, cut into 1-inch pieces

1 cup diced carrots (about 2 medium)

½ cup finely chopped onion (1 medium)

½ cup halved pitted ripe olives

2 cloves garlic, finely chopped

1 carton (32 oz) chicken broth (4 cups)

1 can (14.5 oz) Italian-style diced tomatoes, undrained

½ cup uncooked small pasta shells (2 oz)

1 In 3½- to 4-quart slow cooker, mix all ingredients except pasta.

2 Cover and cook on Low heat setting 8 to 10 hours.

3 About 30 minutes before serving, stir in pasta. Increase heat setting to High. Cover and cook 20 to 30 minutes longer or until pasta is tender.

1 Serving: Calories 210; Total Fat 6g (Saturated Fat 1.5g, Trans Fat 0g); Cholesterol 85mg; Sodium 900mg; Total Carbohydrate 17g (Dietary Fiber 2g); Protein 22g **Exchanges:** 1 Starch, ½ Vegetable, 2½ Very Lean Meat, 1 Fat **Carbohydrate Choices:** 1

Pasta Point

The night before, cut up all of the components for this slow-cooker soup. Package them separately and refrigerate. In the morning, assemble the soup in minutes.

Pasta Pairing

Thick slices of hearty Italian bread drizzled with olive oil complete this Italian soup meal.

chicken and spinach tortellini soup

prep time: 30 Minutes • **start to finish:** 30 Minutes • 5 servings

1 tablespoon olive or vegetable oil

5 medium green onions, chopped (⅓ cup)

⅓ cup julienne carrots (from 10-oz bag)

2 cloves garlic, finely chopped

6 cups chicken broth (from two 32-oz cartons)

2 cups shredded cooked chicken

1 cup frozen cheese-filled tortellini

¼ teaspoon ground nutmeg, if desired

⅛ teaspoon pepper

3 cups chopped fresh spinach

1 In 4½- to 5-quart Dutch oven or saucepan, heat oil over medium-high heat. Cook onions, carrots and garlic in oil 3 to 4 minutes, stirring frequently, until onions are softened.

2 Stir in broth and chicken. Heat to boiling. Stir in tortellini; reduce heat to medium. Cover; cook 3 to 5 minutes or until tortellini is tender.

3 Stir in nutmeg, pepper and spinach. Cover; cook 2 to 3 minutes longer or until spinach is hot.

1 Serving: Calories 230; Total Fat 9g (Saturated Fat 3g; Trans Fat 0g); Cholesterol 80mg; Sodium 1310mg; Total Carbohydrate 11g (Dietary Fiber 1g); Protein 26g **Exchanges:** ½ Starch, ½ Vegetable, 3½ Very Lean Meat, 1½ Fat **Carbohydrate Choices:** 1

••

Improvise

Dried cheese-filled tortellini can be used in place of the frozen tortellini by adjusting the cooking time according to the package instructions. You can also substitute shredded carrots for the julienne carrots.

chicken pasta soup

prep time: 40 Minutes • start to finish: 40 Minutes • 6 servings

2 teaspoons butter

3 boneless skinless chicken breasts, cut into thin strips

1 package (8 oz) sliced fresh mushrooms (3 cups)

3 cans (14 oz each) fat-free chicken broth with 33% less sodium

1½ cups uncooked medium pasta shells (4 oz)

1 cup sliced yellow summer squash or zucchini

½ cup chopped red bell pepper

1 teaspoon Italian seasoning

1 In 4-quart nonstick saucepan or Dutch oven, heat butter over medium heat until hot. Cook chicken and mushrooms in butter, stirring occasionally, until chicken is no longer pink in center. Stir in remaining ingredients. Heat to boiling.

2 Reduce heat to low; simmer 10 to 13 minutes, until pasta is tender.

1 Serving : Calories 190; Total Fat 4g (Saturated Fat 1.5g; Trans Fat 0g); Cholesterol 40mg; Sodium 500mg; Total Carbohydrate 19g (Dietary Fiber 1g); Protein 20g **Exchanges:** 1 Starch, 1 Vegetable, 2 Very Lean Meat, ½ Fat **Carbohydrate Choices:** 1

Improvise

Rotisserie chicken can be used in place of the raw chicken. It's not necessary to cook the chicken with the mushrooms; instead, chop and add it with the rest of the ingredients.

ginger chicken noodle soup

prep time: 20 Minutes • start to finish: 50 Minutes • 5 servings

- 1 pound skinless, boneless chicken breast halves, cut into 1-inch pieces
- 1 teaspoon canola oil
- 3 medium carrots, sliced
- 5¼ cups reduced-sodium chicken broth
- 1 cup water
- 2 tablespoons rice vinegar
- 1 tablespoon reduced-sodium soy sauce
- 2 to 3 teaspoons grated fresh ginger or ½ to ¾ teaspoon ground ginger
- ¼ teaspoon black pepper
- 2 ounces soba (buckwheat noodles), coarsely broken
- 1 package (9 oz) frozen Sugar Snap Peas
- Reduced-sodium soy sauce (optional)

1 In a Dutch oven cook chicken, half at a time, in hot oil just until browned. Drain off fat. Return all of the chicken to Dutch oven. Add carrots, chicken broth, the water, rice vinegar, the 1 tablespoon soy sauce, ginger, and pepper. Bring to a boil; reduce heat. Cover and simmer for 20 minutes.

2 Add uncooked noodles to soup. Return to a boil; reduce heat. Simmer, uncovered, for 8 to 10 minutes or until noodles are tender.

3 Meanwhile, prepare peas according to package directions. Stir peas into soup just before serving. If desired, serve with additional soy sauce.

4 Slow-Cooker Directions: In a large skillet cook chicken, half at a time, in hot oil just until browned. Using a slotted spoon, transfer chicken to a 3½- to 4-quart slow cooker. Add carrots, chicken broth, the water, rice vinegar, the 1 tablespoon soy sauce, ginger, and pepper. Cover and cook on low-heat setting for 4 to 6 hours or on high-heat setting for 2 to 3 hours.

5 If using low-heat setting, turn to high-heat setting. Stir in uncooked noodles. Cover and cook for 10 to 15 minutes more or until noodles are tender. Prepare peas according to package directions. Add peas to soup and serve as above.

1 Serving: Calories 210 (Calories from Fat 20); Total Fat 2g (Saturated Fat 0.5g, Trans Fat 0g); Cholesterol 55mg; Sodium 880mg; Total Carbohydrate 17g (Dietary Fiber 3g, Sugars 6g); Protein 28g **Exchanges:** 1 Starch, 1 Vegetable, 3 Lean Meat **Carbohydrate Choices:** 1

Jazz Up a Jar of Sauce

We all have a favorite pasta sauce that we have in the pantry for occasions that require a quick and easy meal. Why not jazz up that jar of sauce with one or two tasty ingredients that you also might have on hand? Just take a jar of your favorite pasta sauce and add one or more of the following ingredients to make it your own. Then simmer and serve the sauce with your favorite cooked pasta.

- Cooked, crumbled ground beef, Italian sausage or turkey sausage
- Diced pepperoni or cooked meatballs
- Cooked shrimp or crabmeat
- Sliced ripe olives
- Sliced fresh mushrooms

- Diced bell pepper or green onions
- Frozen whole kernel corn
- Chopped fresh basil or oregano
- Chopped fresh tomato
- Sliced canned artichoke hearts
- Sliced roasted red bell peppers (from a jar)

asian pork and noodle soup

prep time: 30 Minutes • start to finish: 30 Minutes • 5 servings

1 lb boneless pork loin, cut into ½-inch pieces

2 cloves garlic, finely chopped

2 teaspoons finely chopped gingerroot

3½ cups chicken broth (from 32-oz carton)

2 cups water

2 tablespoons soy sauce

2 cups uncooked fine egg noodles (4 oz)

1 medium carrot, sliced (½ cup)

1 small red bell pepper, chopped (½ cup)

2 cups fresh baby spinach leaves

1 Spray 3-quart saucepan with cooking spray; heat over medium-high heat. Add pork, garlic and gingerroot; cook 3 to 5 minutes, stirring frequently, until pork is browned.

2 Stir in broth, water and soy sauce. Heat to boiling. Reduce heat; simmer uncovered 5 minutes.

3 Stir in noodles, carrot and bell pepper. Simmer uncovered about 10 minutes, stirring occasionally, until noodles are tender and pork is no longer pink in center. Stir in spinach; cook until hot.

1 Serving: Calories 230; Total Fat 6g (Saturated Fat 2g; Trans Fat 0g); Cholesterol 55mg; Sodium 1140mg; Total Carbohydrate 19g (Dietary Fiber 1g); Protein 25g **Exchanges:** 1 Starch, ½ Vegetable, 3 Very Lean Meat, 1 Fat **Carbohydrate Choices:** 1

Pasta Point

This soup is nutrient dense from the meat and all the vegetables. Plus, green leafy vegetables such as spinach are a good source of vitamins and minerals.

turkey soup with orzo

prep time: 15 Minutes • **start to finish:** 45 Minutes • 6 servings

2 tablespoons olive oil

1 medium onion, chopped (½ cup)

1 medium carrot, finely chopped (½ cup)

1 medium stalk celery, finely chopped

2 cloves garlic, crushed, finely chopped

2 cartons (32 oz each) chicken broth (8 cups)

1 tablespoon chopped fresh sage leaves, if desired

1 bay leaf

2 cups green beans, cut into 1-inch pieces

1 sweet potato, peeled, diced

½ cup uncooked small pasta, such as orzo or pastina

3 cups diced cooked turkey

1 In Dutch oven or large saucepan, heat oil over medium heat. Add onion, carrot, celery and garlic. Reduce heat to medium-low; cook uncovered 6 to 8 minutes, until vegetables are tender.

2 Add chicken broth, sage and bay leaf. Heat to boiling. Add green beans, sweet potato and pasta. Reduce heat to medium-low; cook uncovered about 10 minutes or until vegetables are tender and pasta is cooked. Stir in turkey. Remove from heat. Cover and let stand 5 to 7 minutes. Remove bay leaf.

1 Serving: Calories 250; Total Fat 9g (Saturated Fat 1.5g, Trans Fat 0g); Cholesterol 75mg; Sodium 1310mg; Total Carbohydrate 20g (Dietary Fiber 3g); Protein 22g **Exchanges:** 1 Starch, 1 Vegetable, 2½ Lean Meat **Carbohydrate Choices:** 1

Improvise

Three cups leftover cooked Thanksgiving side vegetables can be used in place of the fresh vegetables.

turkey-spaetzle soup

prep time: 25 Minutes • start to finish: 25 Minutes • 6 servings

2   tablespoons vegetable oil

1   large onion, finely chopped
    (1 cup)

1   medium carrot, finely
    chopped (½ cup)

1   medium stalk celery, finely
    chopped (½ cup)

1   clove garlic, finely chopped

¼   cup all-purpose flour

1   tablespoon chopped fresh
    or 2 teaspoons dried
    thyme leaves

¼   teaspoon pepper

2   cups diced cooked turkey

6   cups chicken broth
    (from two 32-oz cartons)

1   package (12 oz)
    frozen spaetzle

    Chopped fresh parsley,
    if desired

1 In 4-quart Dutch oven or saucepan, heat oil over medium-high heat. Add onion, carrot, celery and garlic; cook about 2 minutes, stirring frequently, until crisp-tender.

2 Gradually stir in flour, thyme and pepper; cook and stir about 1 minute. Stir in turkey and broth; heat to boiling.

3 Stir in frozen spaetzle. Cook 2 to 3 minutes, stirring occasionally, until spaetzle are tender. Sprinkle with parsley.

1 Serving: Calories 240; Total Fat 10g (Saturated Fat 2.5g; Trans Fat 0g); Cholesterol 70mg; Sodium 1180mg; Total Carbohydrate 17g (Dietary Fiber 2g); Protein 21g **Exchanges:** 1 Starch, 2½ Lean Meat, ½ Fat **Carbohydrate Choices:** 1

Improvise

If you prefer, substitute 3 cups frozen egg noodles (from 16-ounce bag) for the spaetzle.

slow-cooker beef and tortellini soup

prep time: 20 Minutes • **start to finish:** 8 Hours 50 Minutes • 6 servings

1 lb beef stew meat

1 large onion, chopped (¾ cup)

1 large carrot, chopped (¾ cup)

1 medium stalk celery, chopped (½ cup)

2 cloves garlic, finely chopped

2 teaspoons sugar

1 can (14.5 oz) diced tomatoes, undrained

2 cans (10.5 oz each) condensed beef broth

1 teaspoon dried basil leaves

2 cups frozen cheese-filled tortellini (from 19-oz bag)

1 cup frozen cut green beans (from 12-oz bag)

1 Spray 3½- to 4-quart slow cooker with cooking spray. In slow cooker, place beef, onion, carrot, celery, garlic, sugar, tomatoes and broth in order listed.

2 Cover; cook on Low heat setting 8 to 9 hours.

3 Stir in basil, frozen tortellini and green beans. Increase heat setting to High. Cover; cook 30 minutes longer or until beans are tender.

1 Serving: Calories 310; Total Fat 14g (Saturated Fat 5g; Trans Fat 1g); Cholesterol 100mg; Sodium 710mg; Total Carbohydrate 22g (Dietary Fiber 3g); Protein 26g **Exchanges:** 1 Starch, 1 Vegetable, 3 Lean Meat, 1 Fat **Carbohydrate Choices:** 1½

Pasta Point

Top each serving with a teaspoon of refrigerated basil pesto.

cheesy lasagna soup

prep time: 40 Minutes • **start to finish:** 40 Minutes • 6 servings

1 lb lean (at least 80%) ground beef

1 medium onion, sliced

2 large green bell peppers, cut into 1-inch pieces

2 cloves garlic, finely chopped

2 cups water

2 cans (14.5 oz each) diced tomatoes with Italian herbs, undrained

1 can (6 oz) tomato paste

2 cups uncooked mini lasagna (mafalda) noodles (4 oz)

1 tablespoon packed brown sugar

1½ teaspoons Italian seasoning

¼ teaspoon pepper

1½ cups Italian-seasoned croutons

1½ cups shredded reduced-fat mozzarella cheese

1 In 4-quart saucepan or Dutch oven, cook beef, onion, bell peppers and garlic over medium heat 8 to 10 minutes, stirring occasionally, until beef is thoroughly cooked and onion is tender; drain.

2 Stir in water, tomatoes and tomato paste. Stir in noodles, brown sugar, Italian seasoning and pepper. Heat to boiling; reduce heat. Cover; simmer about 10 minutes, stirring occasionally, until noodles are tender.

3 Set oven control to broil. Pour hot soup into 6 ovenproof soup bowls or casseroles. Top each with ¼ cup croutons and ¼ cup cheese. Broil soup with tops 3 to 4 inches from heat 1 to 2 minutes or until cheese is melted.

1 Serving: Calories 500; Total Fat 16g (Saturated Fat 7g, Trans Fat 1g); Cholesterol 65mg; Sodium 820mg; Total Carbohydrate 59g (Dietary Fiber 6g); Protein 29g **Exchanges:** 2 Starch, 1½ Other Carbohydrate, 1 Vegetable, 2 Lean Meat, 1 Medium-Fat Meat, 1 Fat **Carbohydrate Choices:** 4

Pasta Point

This soup is great when made ahead and reheated; the flavor improves with age. Make the soup through step 2. Cool and store, covered and refrigerated, up to 3 days. Just before serving, reheat the soup and then broil with croutons and cheese.

chili mac soup

prep time: 25 Minutes • **start to finish:** 25 Minutes • 6 servings

1   lb lean (at least 80%) ground beef

1   medium onion, chopped (½ cup)

¼   cup chopped green bell pepper

5   cups hot water

1   box Hamburger Helper chili macaroni

1   teaspoon chili powder

½   teaspoon garlic salt

2   cups diced tomatoes (from 28-oz can)

1   can (11 oz) vacuum-packed whole kernel corn with red and green peppers, undrained

2   tablespoons sliced pitted ripe olives

1 In 4-quart Dutch oven or saucepan, cook ground beef, onion and bell pepper over medium-high heat 5 to 7 minutes, stirring occasionally, until beef is thoroughly cooked. Drain beef in colander over a small bowl.

2 Stir in hot water, sauce mix (from Hamburger Helper box), chili powder, garlic salt and tomatoes. Heat to boiling, stirring occasionally.

3 Reduce heat; cover and simmer 5 minutes, stirring occasionally. Stir in the uncooked pasta (from Hamburger Helper box), corn and olives. Cover and cook 10 minutes longer, stirring occasionally.

1 Serving: Calories 330; Total Fat 10g (Saturated Fat 3.5g; Trans Fat 0.5g); Cholesterol 45mg; Sodium 990mg; Total Carbohydrate 40g (Dietary Fiber 3g); Protein 18g **Exchanges:** 2½ Starch, 1½ Medium-Fat Meat, ½ Fat **Carbohydrate Choices:** 2½

Pasta Point

Ladle this soup over a mound of corn chips and shredded taco cheese, or sprinkle each serving of soup with corn chips or coarsely crushed tortilla chips.

thai beef noodle bowls

prep time: 50 Minutes • start to finish: 50 Minutes • 6 servings

1 tablespoon vegetable oil

1 lb boneless beef top sirloin steak, thinly sliced across grain

½ teaspoon pepper

¼ teaspoon salt

1 medium onion, thinly sliced (1 cup)

2 tablespoons finely chopped gingerroot

2 jalapeño chiles, seeded, chopped

2 large cloves garlic, finely chopped

3 cups water

3 cups reduced-sodium chicken broth

2 tablespoons reduced-sodium soy sauce

1½ cups thinly sliced Chinese (napa) cabbage

1 package (8 oz) uncooked tofu shirataki noodles, spaghetti style, drained, rinsed well

6 fresh mint leaves

2 tablespoons chopped fresh cilantro

6 tablespoons thinly sliced green onions (5 or 6 medium)

1 lime, cut into 6 pieces

1 In 5-quart Dutch oven or saucepan, heat oil over medium-high heat. Sprinkle beef with pepper and salt. Cook beef in oil, stirring occasionally, until browned on all sides. Using slotted spoon, remove from pan to bowl (leave juices in pan). Cover beef and keep warm.

2 Reduce heat to medium. Add onion, gingerroot and chiles. Cook 5 to 7 minutes, stirring occasionally, until onion is tender. Add garlic; cook 1 minute, scraping up any beef bits from bottom of pan.

3 Add water, chicken broth and soy sauce; heat to boiling. Add cabbage and noodles, stirring well to separate noodles. Add beef; cook uncovered, stirring occasionally, until heated through. Top each serving with 1 mint leaf, 1 teaspoon cilantro, 1 tablespoon onion and 1 piece lime.

1 Serving: Calories 170; Total Fat 5g (Saturated Fat 1g; Trans Fat 0g); Cholesterol 50mg; Sodium 590mg; Total Carbohydrate 7g (Dietary Fiber 2g); Protein 22g **Exchanges:** ½ Other Carbohydrate, ½ Vegetable, 3 Very Lean Meat, ½ Fat **Carbohydrate Choices:** ½

Pasta Point

Peeling fresh gingerroot requires nothing more than a small spoon. Use the inside of a spoon to scrape away the thin skin, then thinly slice and mince.

spicy angel hair pasta and meatball soup

prep time: 25 Minutes • **start to finish:** 25 Minutes • 6 servings

1 tablespoon olive oil

1 medium onion, chopped (½ cup)

3 cans (14.5 oz each) diced tomatoes with Italian herbs, undrained

3½ cups chicken broth (from 32-oz carton)

1 tablespoon Sriracha sauce

½ teaspoon garlic salt

4 oz uncooked angel hair (cappellini) pasta, broken into 2-inch pieces

24 frozen cooked meatballs (from 24-oz bag)

1 In 5-quart Dutch oven or saucepan, heat oil over medium-high heat. Cook onion in oil about 3 minutes, stirring occasionally, until tender. Stir in tomatoes, broth, Sriracha sauce and garlic salt. Heat to boiling, stirring occasionally.

2 Stir in pasta and meatballs. Heat to boiling; reduce heat. Cover and simmer about 6 minutes, stirring occasionally, until pasta is tender and meatballs are thoroughly heated.

1 Serving: Calories 460; Total Fat 19g (Saturated Fat 6g; Trans Fat 1g); Cholesterol 120mg; Sodium 1810mg; Total Carbohydrate 41g (Dietary Fiber 4g); Protein 30g **Exchanges:** 2 Starch, ½ Other Carbohydrate, 2 Lean Meat, 1½ Medium-Fat Meat, 1 Fat **Carbohydrate Choices:** 3

Pasta Point

Sriracha is a hot chili sauce, made from ground chiles, vinegar, garlic, sugar and salt. It's thicker and not quite as hot as hot sauces typically used for Buffalo wings. Look for it near the ethnic ingredients at the grocery store or at Asian markets.

easy beef and pasta soup

prep time: 35 Minutes • **start to finish:** 35 Minutes • 8 servings

1 lb lean (at least 80%) ground beef

1 medium onion, chopped (½ cup)

1 box Hamburger Helper beef pasta

6 cups water

1½ teaspoons chopped fresh or ½ teaspoon dried basil leaves

⅛ teaspoon pepper

2 cloves garlic, crushed

1 can (4 oz) mushroom stems and pieces, drained

2 tablespoons chopped fresh parsley

1 In 4-quart Dutch oven or saucepan, cook beef and onion over medium heat, stirring occasionally, until beef is browned; drain.

2 Stir in sauce mix (from Hamburger Helper box), water, basil, pepper and garlic. Heat to boiling, stirring frequently; reduce heat. Cover and simmer 10 minutes, stirring occasionally.

3 Stir in pasta (from Hamburger Helper box) and mushrooms. Heat to boiling; reduce heat. Cover and simmer 10 minutes, stirring occasionally. Sprinkle with parsley.

1 Serving: Calories 170; Total Fat 7g (Saturated Fat 2.5g, Trans Fat 0g); Cholesterol 35mg; Sodium 420mg; Total Carbohydrate 15g (Dietary Fiber 0g); Protein 12g **Exchanges:** 1 Starch, 1 Medium-Fat Meat, ½ Fat **Carbohydrate Choices:** 1

Improvise

For a heartier, robust flavor, add a splash of dry red wine to the soup when adding the pasta and mushrooms.

Pasta Pairing

Serve this soup with a crisp cucumber and red onion salad. Marinate the vegetables in seasoned rice vinegar in the refrigerator until ready to serve.

minestrone with italian sausage

prep time: 45 Minutes • start to finish: 45 Minutes • 7 servings

1 tablespoon olive or vegetable oil

1 lb bulk sweet Italian pork sausage

2 medium carrots, coarsely chopped (1 cup)

1 medium onion, chopped (½ cup)

2 teaspoons dried basil leaves

2 teaspoons finely chopped garlic

5¼ cups beef broth (from two 32-oz cartons)

1 can (14.5 oz) diced tomatoes, undrained

1 can (15.5 oz) great northern beans, drained, rinsed

1 cup uncooked elbow macaroni (4 oz)

1 medium zucchini, cut in half lengthwise, then cut crosswise into ¼-inch slices (1 cup)

1 cup frozen cut green beans

1 In 5-quart Dutch oven or saucepan, heat oil over medium-high heat. Add sausage, carrots, onion, basil and garlic. Cook 5 to 7 minutes, stirring frequently, until sausage is no longer pink; drain.

2 Stir broth, tomatoes and great northern beans into sausage mixture. Heat to boiling; reduce heat to medium-low. Cover and cook 7 to 8 minutes, stirring occasionally.

3 Stir in macaroni, zucchini and green beans. Heat to boiling over medium-high heat. Cook 5 to 6 minutes, stirring occasionally, until vegetables are hot and macaroni is tender.

1 Serving : Calories 380; Total Fat 16g (Saturated Fat 5g; Trans Fat 0g); Cholesterol 25mg; Sodium 1400mg; Total Carbohydrate 38g (Dietary Fiber 6g); Protein 20g **Exchanges:** 2 Starch, 1 Vegetable, 1½ Medium-Fat Meat, 1½ Fat **Carbohydrate Choices:** 2½

Improvise

To make this a meatless soup, use 1 additional can (15.5 ounces) great northern beans (or your favorite canned beans) instead of the sausage, and substitute vegetable broth for the beef broth.

rigatoni pizza stew

prep time: 30 Minutes • **start to finish:** 30 Minutes • **4 servings**

1 lb Italian sausage links, cut into ¼-inch slices

1 can (14.5 oz) Italian-style stewed tomatoes, undrained

1¾ cups beef broth (from 32-oz carton)

1 cup water

¼ cup tomato paste with Italian herbs (from 6-oz can)

2 medium carrots, cut into ½-inch slices (1 cup)

1 medium onion, coarsely chopped (½ cup)

1½ cups uncooked rigatoni pasta (4½ oz)

1 medium zucchini, cut lengthwise in half, then cut crosswise into ¼-inch slices (2 cups)

½ cup shredded mozzarella cheese

1 Spray 4-quart saucepan or Dutch oven with cooking spray; heat over medium heat. Add sausage; cook, stirring occasionally, until no longer pink. Drain.

2 Stir in tomatoes, broth, water, tomato paste, carrots and onion. Heat to boiling. Reduce heat to medium-low; cook uncovered about 10 minutes or until carrots are tender.

3 Stir in pasta and zucchini. Cook uncovered 10 to 12 minutes, stirring occasionally, until pasta is tender. Sprinkle each serving with 2 tablespoons cheese.

1 Serving: Calories 560; Total Fat 27g (Saturated Fat 10g; Trans Fat 0g); Cholesterol 55mg; Sodium 2170mg; Total Carbohydrate 52g (Dietary Fiber 5g); Protein 28g **Exchanges:** 2½ Starch, 3 Vegetable, 2 High-Fat Meat, 2 Fat **Carbohydrate Choices:** 3½

Improvise

Italian turkey sausage can be used in place of the regular sausage. Or for the pepperoni pizza lovers in your family, substitute sliced pepperoni; skip step 1 and stir the pepperoni into the tomato mixture in step 2.

slow-cooker italian tortellini stew

prep time: 15 Minutes • start to finish: 6 Hours 15 Minutes • 8 servings

1 small onion, finely chopped (⅓ cup)

2 medium zucchini, cut lengthwise in half, then cut crosswise into 1-inch slices

3½ cups vegetable or chicken broth

1 can (28 oz) crushed or diced tomatoes, undrained

1 can (15 oz) great northern beans, drained, rinsed

¼ teaspoon salt

¼ teaspoon pepper

1 tablespoon dried basil leaves

1 package (7 oz) dried cheese-filled tortellini

1 In 4- to 6-quart slow cooker, combine all ingredients except basil and tortellini; mix well.

2 Cover; cook on Low heat setting 6 to 8 hours.

3 About 20 minutes before serving, stir basil and tortellini into stew. Increase heat setting to High; cover and cook 20 minutes longer or until tortellini are tender.

1 Serving: Calories 310; Total Fat 6g (Saturated Fat 1.5g, Trans Fat 0g); Cholesterol 40mg; Sodium 1100mg; Total Carbohydrate 51g (Dietary Fiber 6g); Protein 12g **Exchanges:** 2 Starch, 1 Other Carbohydrate, 1 Vegetable, ½ Lean Meat, ½ Fat **Carbohydrate Choices:** 3½

Pasta Points

Cheese-filled tortellini is available both dried and refrigerated. Look for a freshness date on the refrigerated variety. This recipe uses the dried type, so if you use refrigerated tortellini, it will cook faster.

Made with vegetable broth, this stew is entirely meatless. The combination of beans, pasta and cheese provides complete protein.

Pasta Pairing

Ladle the stew into sturdy serving bowls, and sprinkle with grated Parmesan cheese and chopped fresh basil.

slow-cooker tomato rotini soup

prep time: 15 Minutes • **start to finish:** 8 Hours 30 Minutes • 6 servings

4 cups vegetable broth

4 cups tomato juice

1 tablespoon dried basil leaves

1 teaspoon salt

½ teaspoon dried oregano leaves

¼ teaspoon pepper

2 medium carrots, sliced (1 cup)

2 medium stalks celery, chopped (1 cup)

1 medium onion, chopped (½ cup)

1 cup sliced fresh mushrooms

2 cloves garlic, finely chopped

1 can (28 oz) diced tomatoes, undrained

1½ cups uncooked rotini pasta (4½ oz)

Shredded Parmesan cheese, if desired

1 Spray 5- to 6-quart slow cooker with cooking spray. Mix all ingredients except pasta and cheese in slow cooker.

2 Cover; cook on Low heat setting 8 to 9 hours or until vegetables are tender.

3 Stir in pasta. Increase heat setting to High. Cook 15 to 20 minutes longer or until pasta is tender. Sprinkle each serving with cheese.

1 Serving: Calories 180; Total Fat 1g (Saturated Fat 0g; Trans Fat 0g); Cholesterol 0mg; Sodium 1670mg; Total Carbohydrate 37g (Dietary Fiber 5g); Protein 6g **Exchanges:** 2 Starch, 1 Vegetable **Carbohydrate Choices:** 2½

slow-cooker italian vegetable soup

prep time: 5 Minutes • **start to finish:** 8 Hours 5 Minutes • 6 servings

- 2 cans (19 oz) cannellini beans, drained
- 1 package (16 oz) frozen mixed vegetables
- 1 can (14.5 oz) diced tomatoes with basil, garlic and oregano, undrained
- 1 bottle (12 oz) vegetable juice cocktail
- ½ teaspoon salt
- 1 cup water
- ½ cup uncooked penne or mostaccioli pasta (1½ oz)
- ¼ cup basil pesto

1 In 3- to 4-quart slow cooker, combine all ingredients except penne and pesto; mix well.

2 Cover; cook on Low setting 8 to 9 hours.

3 About 20 minutes before serving, stir penne into soup. Increase heat setting to High; cover and cook 15 to 20 minutes longer or until penne is tender.

4 To serve, top individual servings with 2 teaspoons pesto.

1 Serving: Calories 290; Total Fat 6g (Saturated Fat 1g, Trans Fat 0g); Cholesterol 0mg; Sodium 920mg; Total Carbohydrate 46g (Dietary Fiber 11g); Protein 14g **Exchanges:** 2½ Starch, 1 Vegetable, ½ Very Lean Meat, 1 Fat **Carbohydrate Choices:** 3

Improvise

Great northern beans can be used in place of the cannellini beans. The can sizes will vary, but in this soup, those differences won't matter.

Pasta Points

Acidic ingredients such as tomatoes and vegetable juice keep vegetables from softening too much during all-day simmering. A garnish of bright green pesto freshens each serving of long-cooked soup.

Don't be fooled into adding more pasta; ½ cup looks skimpy when you stir it in, but as it cooks, it turns into the right proportion for the soup.

slow-cooker lentil and pasta stew

prep time: 10 minutes • **start to finish:** 10 hours 35 minutes • **4 servings**

¾ cup dried lentils, sorted, rinsed

2 medium stalks celery, sliced (1 cup)

½ cup coarsely chopped green bell pepper

3½ cups vegetable broth

1 can (11.5 oz) vegetable juice

⅓ cup uncooked rosamarina or orzo pasta (2 oz)

1 teaspoon dried thyme leaves

1 In 3½- to 4-quart slow cooker, mix lentils, celery, bell pepper and broth.

2 Cover; cook on Low heat setting 10 to 12 hours.

3 Stir vegetable juice, pasta and thyme into stew. Increase heat setting to High. Cover; cook 25 to 30 minutes longer or until pasta is tender.

1 Serving: Calories 220; Total Fat 1g (Saturated Fat 0g; Trans Fat 0g); Cholesterol 0mg; Sodium 1110mg; Total Carbohydrate 40g (Dietary Fiber 8g); Protein 12g **Exchanges:** 1½ Starch, 1 Other Carbohydrate, 1 Very Lean Meat **Carbohydrate Choices:** 2½

Pasta Point

Lentils come in many colors, including brown, green, red and yellow. You can find brown lentils in most supermarkets, but you may have to look in a specialty market to find the green, red and yellow varieties.

ravioli and eggplant stew

prep time: 55 Minutes • **start to finish:** 55 Minutes • **4 servings**

3 tablespoons olive or vegetable oil

2 cups cubed eggplant

1 can (14.5 oz) Italian-style stewed tomatoes, undrained

1½ teaspoons chopped fresh or ½ teaspoon dried basil leaves

1 cup water

1 medium zucchini, cut in half lengthwise, then crosswise into ½-inch slices (2 cups)

1 package (9 oz) refrigerated cheese-filled ravioli

1 cup shredded fresh Parmesan cheese

1 In 12-inch skillet, heat oil over medium-high heat. Add eggplant; cook 5 minutes, stirring occasionally. Stir in tomatoes and basil. Heat to boiling. Reduce heat; cover and simmer about 15 minutes, stirring once or twice, until eggplant is tender.

2 Stir in water, zucchini and ravioli. Heat to boiling. Reduce heat; cover and simmer 10 minutes, stirring once or twice, until ravioli are tender.

3 Sprinkle with cheese. Cover; simmer about 5 minutes longer or until cheese is melted.

1 Serving: Calories 370; Total Fat 22g (Saturated Fat 8g; Trans Fat 0g); Cholesterol 75mg; Sodium 1100mg; Total Carbohydrate 25g (Dietary Fiber 3g); Protein 17g **Exchanges:** 1 Starch, 2½ Vegetable, 1 Lean Meat, 3½ Fat **Carbohydrate Choices:** 1½

. . . .

Improvise

All flavors of refrigerated filled ravioli can be used. Try mushroom or chicken for a change of pace!

. . . .

Pasta Point

You can cut up the eggplant ahead of time. But be sure to either brush it with a little lemon juice or dip it in 1 quart cold water mixed with 3 tablespoons lemon juice to prevent the flesh from discoloring.

italian winter stew with vermicelli

prep time: 30 Minutes • **start to finish:** 30 Minutes • 4 servings

½ cup 1-inch pieces uncooked vermicelli or small pasta shells (2 oz)

4 teaspoons olive oil

2 medium onions, chopped (1 cup)

½ medium green bell pepper, chopped (½ cup)

1 medium zucchini, cut in half lengthwise, then crosswise into thin slices (about 1½ cups)

1 can (14.5 oz) diced tomatoes with garlic, oregano and basil, undrained

1¾ cups vegetable or beef-flavored broth (from 32-oz carton)

1 teaspoon Italian seasoning

1 can (15 oz) red kidney beans, drained, rinsed

2 tablespoons chopped fresh parsley

1 Cook and drain vermicelli as directed on package; cover to keep warm.

2 Meanwhile, spray 4-quart Dutch oven or saucepan with cooking spray. Add 1 teaspoon of the oil; heat over medium-high heat. Add onions and bell pepper; cook 5 minutes, stirring occasionally.

3 Stir in zucchini, tomatoes, broth and Italian seasoning. Heat to boiling over high heat. Stir in kidney beans; return just to boiling. Reduce heat to medium; cook 10 minutes.

4 Add vermicelli, parsley and remaining 3 teaspoons oil to stew; stir gently to mix.

1 Serving: Calories 270; Total Fat 6g (Saturated Fat 1g; Trans Fat 0g); Cholesterol 0mg; Sodium 820mg; Total Carbohydrate 46g (Dietary Fiber 10g); Protein 14g **Exchanges:** 3 Starch, 1 Vegetable, 1 Fat **Carbohydrate Choices:** 2½

black bean and salsa noodle soup

prep time: 20 Minutes • start to finish: 20 Minutes • 6 servings

3 cans (14 oz each) vegetable broth

1 jar (16 oz) chunky-style salsa

1 can (15 oz) black beans, drained, rinsed

1 can (11 oz) whole kernel corn, drained

1 package (5 oz) Japanese curly noodles or 5 oz uncooked spaghetti

⅓ cup chopped fresh cilantro

1 tablespoon lime juice

1 teaspoon chili powder

¼ teaspoon ground cumin

¼ teaspoon pepper

2 tablespoons shredded Parmesan cheese

1 In 4-quart Dutch oven or saucepan, heat broth to boiling. Stir in remaining ingredients except cheese; reduce heat to medium.

2 Cook 5 to 6 minutes, stirring occasionally, until noodles are tender. Sprinkle with cheese.

1 Serving: Calories 260; Total Fat 2g (Saturated Fat 0.5g; Trans Fat 0g); Cholesterol 0mg; Sodium 1720mg; Total Carbohydrate 52g (Dietary Fiber 8g); Protein 10g **Exchanges:** 2½ Starch, 1 Other Carbohydrate **Carbohydrate Choices:** 3½

••

Improvise

Chopped fresh parsley can be substituted for the cilantro.

••

Pasta Point

Store a bunch of fresh cilantro, stems down, in a glass of water, and cover with a plastic bag. It will keep up to a week if you change the water every 2 or 3 days. When you're ready to use the cilantro, wash it, dry it with paper towels, then chop.

three-alarm spaghetti and pinto bean chili

prep time: 35 Minutes • **start to finish:** 35 Minutes • 4 servings

1 tablespoon vegetable oil

1 large onion, chopped (1 cup)

1 medium green bell pepper, chopped (1 cup)

3 cups water

½ cup taco sauce

2 teaspoons chili powder

½ teaspoon salt

¼ teaspoon ground cinnamon

2 cans (10 oz each) diced tomatoes and green chiles, undrained

4 oz uncooked spaghetti, broken into thirds (1½ cups)

1 can (15 oz) pinto beans, drained, rinsed

Sour cream, if desired

Jalapeño chiles, if desired

1 In 4-quart Dutch oven or saucepan, heat oil over medium-high heat. Add onion and bell pepper; cook 3 to 5 minutes, stirring occasionally, until crisp-tender.

2 Stir in water, taco sauce, chili powder, salt, cinnamon and tomatoes. Heat to boiling. Reduce heat to medium-low; simmer uncovered 5 minutes, stirring occasionally.

3 Stir in spaghetti and beans. Heat to boiling. Reduce heat to medium; cook uncovered 8 to 10 minutes, stirring occasionally until spaghetti is tender. Garnish each serving with sour cream and jalapeño chiles.

1 Serving: Calories 340; Total Fat 5g (Saturated Fat 1g; Trans Fat 0g); Cholesterol 0mg; Sodium 1000mg; Total Carbohydrate 59g (Dietary Fiber 12g); Protein 14g **Exchanges:** 3½ Starch, 2 Vegetable, ½ Fat **Carbohydrate Choices:** 4

Pasta Point

This chili recipe is based on the well-known Cincinnati chili, which is traditionally chili served over spaghetti. To save time and energy, the spaghetti is cooked right along with this spicy chili.

CHAPTER 5

Oven-Baked Meals

tomato-basil turkey casserole

prep time: 25 Minutes • **start to finish:** 1 Hour 15 Minutes • 6 servings

2 cups uncooked gemelli pasta (8 oz)

2 cups diced cooked turkey

1 jar (26 oz) tomato pasta sauce (any hearty or thick variety)

1 medium zucchini, cut lengthwise in half, then cut crosswise into slices (1½ cups)

1 can (2.25 oz) sliced ripe olives, drained

1 teaspoon dried basil leaves

¼ cup shredded Parmesan cheese

1 Heat oven to 375°F. Spray 2-quart casserole with cooking spray. Cook and drain pasta as directed on package.

2 In casserole, mix pasta and all remaining ingredients except cheese.

3 Cover; bake 30 minutes. Sprinkle with cheese. Bake uncovered 15 to 20 minutes longer or until bubbly and thoroughly heated.

1 Serving: Calories 390; Total Fat 12g (Saturated Fat 3g; Trans Fat 0g); Cholesterol 70mg; Sodium 960mg; Total Carbohydrate 49g (Dietary Fiber 3g); Protein 21g **Exchanges:** 2 Starch, 1 Other Carbohydrate, 2 Lean Meat, 1 Fat **Carbohydrate Choices:** 3

Improvise

Gemelli is a pasta that looks like two strands of spaghetti twisted together. Rotini or penne pasta would work well in this recipe, too.

Pasta Point

When shopping for zucchini, choose small zucchini, which tend to be younger and more tender and have thinner skins. The skin should be a vibrant color and free of blemishes.

chicken fettuccine casserole

prep time: 20 Minutes • **start to finish:** 50 Minutes • 4 servings

1 package (9 oz)
   refrigerated fettuccine

3 tablespoons butter

3 tablespoons
   all-purpose flour

1¾ cups chicken broth
   (from 32-oz carton)

½ cup half-and-half

1½ cups cubed cooked chicken

½ cup oil-packed sun-dried
   tomatoes, drained, cut into
   thin strips

2 slices bacon, crisply
   cooked, crumbled

3 tablespoons shredded
   Parmesan cheese

1 Heat oven to 350°F. Spray 8-inch square (2-quart) glass baking dish with cooking spray. Cook and drain fettuccine as directed on package.

2 Meanwhile, melt butter in 2-quart saucepan over medium heat. Stir in flour. Gradually stir in broth. Heat to boiling, stirring constantly; remove from heat. Stir in half-and-half. Stir in chicken, tomatoes and bacon.

3 Add fettuccine to chicken mixture; toss gently to mix well. Spoon into baking dish. Sprinkle with cheese. Bake uncovered about 30 minutes or until hot in center.

1 Serving: Calories 490; Total Fat 22g (Saturated Fat 10g; Trans Fat 0.5g); Cholesterol 85mg; Sodium 1010mg; Total Carbohydrate 44g (Dietary Fiber 2g); Protein 27g
Exchanges: 2 Starch, ½ Other Carbohydrate, ½ Vegetable, 3 Very Lean Meat, 4 Fat
Carbohydrate Choices: 3

Improvise

This casserole is sure to be a crowd-pleasing winner! You can easily double this recipe and bake it in a 13x9-inch (3-quart) glass baking dish.

You can make this dish up to 8 hours in advance. Cover the unbaked casserole tightly with foil, and refrigerate no longer than 24 hours; uncover before baking. The casserole may need to bake an additional 5 to 10 minutes.

chicken and vegetable tetrazzini

prep time: 20 Minutes • **start to finish:** 50 Minutes • 6 servings

7 oz uncooked whole wheat or multigrain spaghetti, broken into thirds

½ cup frozen shelled edamame (from 10-oz bag)

1 cup 1-inch diagonal pieces fresh asparagus

2 tablespoons butter

1 cup sliced fresh mushrooms (3 oz)

¼ cup all-purpose flour

½ teaspoon salt

¼ teaspoon pepper

1 cup chicken broth (from 32-oz carton)

1 cup fat-free half-and-half

2 tablespoons dry sherry or water

2 cups cubed or shredded deli rotisserie chicken (from 2- to 3-lb chicken)

½ cup chopped orange, yellow or red bell pepper

¼ cup shredded Parmesan or Asiago cheese

1 Heat oven to 350°F. Cook spaghetti as directed on package, adding edamame and asparagus during last 3 minutes of cooking time; drain.

2 Meanwhile, in 2-quart saucepan, melt butter over medium heat. Add mushrooms; cook just until tender. Remove from saucepan with slotted spoon; set aside. Stir flour, salt and pepper into same saucepan. Gradually stir in broth until mixture is smooth. Stir in half-and-half. Heat to boiling, stirring constantly. Boil and stir 1 minute.

3 Add mushrooms, spaghetti and vegetables, sherry, chicken and bell pepper to sauce; stir until combined. Spoon into ungreased 2-quart casserole.

4 Bake uncovered 20 minutes. Sprinkle with cheese; bake about 10 minutes longer or until bubbly in center.

1 Serving: Calories 340; Total Fat 11g (Saturated Fat 5g; Trans Fat 0g); Cholesterol 60mg; Sodium 780mg; Total Carbohydrate 37g (Dietary Fiber 4g); Protein 22g **Exchanges:** 2½ Starch, ½ Vegetable, 2 Lean Meat, ½ Fat **Carbohydrate Choices:** 2½

....

Improvise

Substitute cubed cooked turkey for the chicken and frozen sweet peas for the edamame.

spicy asian chicken and noodle casserole

prep time: 15 Minutes • **start to finish:** 50 Minutes • 4 servings

⅔ cup Thai peanut sauce

⅔ cup chicken broth (from 32-oz carton)

3 tablespoons peanut butter

1 bag (1 lb) frozen broccoli stir-fry vegetables

1 package (7.31 oz) refrigerated cooked stir-fry noodles, separated

2 packages (6 oz each) refrigerated grilled chicken breast strips

¼ cup chow mein noodles

¼ cup chopped peanuts

1 Heat oven to 350°F. Spray 2-quart casserole with cooking spray.

2 In 3-quart saucepan, mix peanut sauce, broth, peanut butter, frozen vegetables and stir-fry noodles. Cook over medium-high heat 5 to 7 minutes, stirring frequently, until hot. Stir in chicken. Spoon into casserole.

3 In small bowl, mix chow mein noodles and peanuts; sprinkle over chicken mixture.

4 Bake uncovered about 30 minutes or until hot. Let stand 5 minutes before serving.

1 Serving: Calories 190; Total Fat 10g (Saturated Fat 4g; Trans Fat 0.5g); Cholesterol 20mg; Sodium 90mg; Total Carbohydrate 21g (Dietary Fiber 1g); Protein 3g **Exchanges:** ½ Starch, 1 Other Carbohydrate, 2 Fat **Carbohydrate Choices:** 1½

Improvise

Look for the stir-fry noodles in the refrigerator section of the grocery store, usually near the produce. If you can't find them, use 2 packages of any flavor of ramen noodles. Cook and drain ramen noodles as directed on package, omitting the seasoning packet.

green chile–chicken lasagna

prep time: 25 Minutes • **start to finish:** 1 Hour 35 Minutes • **10 servings**

1 container (15 oz) ricotta cheese

1 egg

1 cup grated Parmesan cheese

2 cups chopped cooked chicken

2 cans (10 oz each) green enchilada sauce

2 cans (4.5 oz each) chopped green chiles

12 precooked lasagna noodles (shelf stable or frozen), each about 7x3 inches

4 cups shredded mozzarella cheese (16 oz)

1 Heat oven to 350°F. In medium bowl, mix ricotta cheese, egg and ½ cup of the Parmesan cheese; set aside. In another medium bowl, mix chicken, enchilada sauce and chiles.

2 In ungreased 13x9-inch (3-quart) glass baking dish, spread 1 cup of the chicken mixture. Top with 3 uncooked lasagna noodles; press gently into chicken mixture. Spread with ⅔ cup of the ricotta mixture. Sprinkle with 1 cup of the mozzarella cheese. Repeat layers 3 times. Sprinkle with remaining ½ cup Parmesan cheese.

3 Cover; bake 45 minutes. Uncover; bake 10 to 15 minutes longer or until noodles are tender, cheese is bubbly and edges are lightly browned. Let stand 10 minutes before serving.

1 Serving: Calories 420; Total Fat 20g (Saturated Fat 11g; Trans Fat 0g); Cholesterol 90mg; Sodium 880mg; Total Carbohydrate 28g (Dietary Fiber 1g); Protein 33g
Exchanges: 1½ Starch, ½ Other Carbohydrate, 4 Lean Meat, 1 Fat
Carbohydrate Choices: 2

••

Pasta Point

The lasagna noodles won't cover the entire baking dish at first; they expand as they absorb liquid and cook, so when the dish is done, the lasagna will fill the pan. Look for oven-ready lasagna with the rest of the dry pasta in the grocery store.

salsa beef and rotini

prep time: 25 Minutes • start to finish: 1 Hour • 6 servings

1⅓ cups uncooked whole wheat or regular rotini pasta (4 oz)

12 oz extra-lean (at least 90%) ground beef

2 cloves garlic, finely chopped

1 can (15 oz) black beans, drained, rinsed

1 can (14.5 oz) no-salt-added diced tomatoes, undrained

¾ cup chunky-style salsa

1 teaspoon dried oregano leaves

½ teaspoon ground cumin

½ teaspoon chili powder

½ cup shredded reduced-fat Colby–Monterey Jack cheese blend

⅓ cup reduced-fat sour cream

3 medium green onions, sliced (3 tablespoons)

2 teaspoons coarsely chopped fresh cilantro

½ teaspoon grated lime peel

1 Heat oven to 350°F. Cook pasta as directed on package, omitting salt and oil and using minimum cook time; drain and return to saucepan.

2 Meanwhile, in large skillet, cook beef and garlic over medium-high heat 5 to 7 minutes, stirring occasionally, until beef is thoroughly cooked; drain. Stir beef into pasta in saucepan. Stir in beans, tomatoes, salsa, oregano, cumin and chili powder. Transfer mixture to ungreased 1½- or 2-quart casserole.

3 Cover; bake about 30 minutes or until thoroughly heated. Uncover and sprinkle with cheese. Bake about 3 minutes longer or until cheese is melted.

4 In small bowl, stir sour cream, 2 tablespoons of the onions, the cilantro and lime peel. Top each serving with a spoonful of sour cream mixture. Sprinkle with remaining 1 tablespoon onions.

1 Serving : Calories 330; Total Fat 8g (Saturated Fat 3.5g; Trans Fat 0g); Cholesterol 40mg; Sodium 260mg; Total Carbohydrate 42g (Dietary Fiber 9g); Protein 23g
Exchanges: 2½ Starch, ½ Vegetable, 2 Lean Meat **Carbohydrate Choices:** 3

tortilla casserole

prep time: 25 Minutes • **start to finish:** 45 Minutes • 6 servings

1 lb lean (at least 80%) ground beef

1 small onion, chopped (⅓ cup)

1⅓ cups hot water

1 cup chunky-style salsa

½ cup milk

1 box Hamburger Helper™ cheeseburger macaroni

6 flour tortillas (7 or 8 inch)

1½ cups shredded Cheddar cheese

1 Heat oven to 350°F. In 10-inch skillet, cook beef and onion over medium-high heat, stirring occasionally, until beef is browned; drain. Stir in hot water, salsa, milk, uncooked pasta and sauce mix (from Hamburger Helper box). Heat to boiling, stirring occasionally. Reduce heat; cover and simmer about 7 minutes, stirring occasionally, until pasta is tender.

2 Cut tortillas in half. Spread 2 cups beef mixture in ungreased 11x7-inch (2-quart) glass baking dish or shallow 2-quart casserole; top with 6 tortilla halves and ¾ cup cheese. Spread with 2 cups beef mixture; top with remaining tortilla halves. Top with remaining beef mixture and cheese.

3 Bake uncovered 15 to 20 minutes or until hot and cheese is melted.

1 Serving: Calories 530; Total Fat 22g (Saturated Fat 10g, Trans Fat 1.5g); Cholesterol 80mg; Sodium 1500mg; Total Carbohydrate 54g (Dietary Fiber 2g); Protein 28g **Exchanges:** 2½ Starch, 1 Other Carbohydrate, 2 Lean Meat, 1 High-Fat Meat, 1½ Fat **Carbohydrate Choices:** 3½

• •

Improvise

If you like it spicy, use hot salsa and shredded Pepper Jack cheese.

• •

Pasta Point

Store leftover tortillas in a resealable food-storage plastic bag or in plastic wrap in the refrigerator.

chicken and spinach-stuffed shells

prep time: 30 Minutes • **start to finish:** 1 Hour 10 Minutes • 6 servings

18 uncooked jumbo pasta shells

1 container (15 oz) whole-milk ricotta cheese

1 egg, slightly beaten

¼ cup grated Parmesan cheese

2 cups frozen cut-leaf spinach, thawed, squeezed to drain

1 cup chopped cooked chicken

1 jar (26 oz) tomato pasta sauce

2 cups shredded Italian cheese blend

1 Heat oven to 350°F. Cook and drain pasta as directed on package. Rinse with cool water; drain.

2 Meanwhile, in medium bowl, mix ricotta cheese, egg, Parmesan cheese, spinach and chicken.

3 Spread 1 cup of the pasta sauce in bottom of ungreased 13x9-inch (3-quart) glass baking dish. Spoon about 2 tablespoons ricotta mixture into each pasta shell. Arrange shells, filled side up, on sauce in baking dish. Spoon remaining sauce over stuffed shells.

4 Cover dish with foil; bake 30 minutes. Sprinkle with Italian cheese blend. Bake uncovered 5 to 10 minutes longer or until cheese is melted.

1 Serving: Calories 570; Total Fat 28g (Saturated Fat 15g; Trans Fat 0.5g); Cholesterol 120mg; Sodium 1330mg; Total Carbohydrate 48g (Dietary Fiber 4g); Protein 33g **Exchanges:** 3 Starch, 1 Vegetable, 3 Medium-Fat Meat, 2 Fat **Carbohydrate Choices:** 3

Improvise

If you prefer to make this ahead, make as directed through step 3. Cover tightly and refrigerate up to 24 hours. Add 5 to 10 minutes to the first bake time before topping with cheese.

mexican manicotti

prep time: 30 Minutes • **start to finish:** 1 Hour 20 Minutes • 6 servings

12 uncooked manicotti
   pasta shells

1 lb lean (at least 80%)
   ground beef

1 can (6 oz) tomato paste

1 package (1 oz) taco
   seasoning mix

1½ cups water

1 package (3 oz) cream
   cheese, softened

1 egg

1½ cups sour cream (12 oz)

2½ cups shredded sharp
   Cheddar cheese (10 oz)

2 cans (4 oz each) whole
   green chiles, drained,
   chopped

¼ cup chopped fresh cilantro

1 Heat oven to 350°F. Spray 13x9-inch (3-quart) glass baking dish with cooking spray. Cook and drain pasta as directed on package. Rinse with cold water; drain well.

2 Meanwhile, in 10-inch nonstick skillet, cook beef over medium-high heat 5 to 7 minutes, stirring occasionally, until thoroughly cooked; drain. Stir in tomato paste, taco seasoning mix and water. Cook over medium heat 5 to 10 minutes longer, until hot and bubbly.

3 In medium bowl, mix cream cheese, egg, sour cream, 1½ cups of the cheese, the chiles and 2 tablespoons of the cilantro. Spoon about 3 tablespoons cheese mixture into each pasta shell. Spoon about 1 cup beef mixture into baking dish. Arrange shells, filled side up, on beef mixture; top with remaining beef mixture.

4 Cover; bake 40 to 45 minutes or until hot. Uncover; sprinkle remaining 1 cup cheese over shells. Bake 5 minutes longer or until cheese is melted. Sprinkle with remaining 2 tablespoons cilantro.

1 Serving: Calories 700; Total Fat 42g (Saturated Fat 23g; Trans Fat 1.5g); Cholesterol 175mg; Sodium 1390mg; Total Carbohydrate 45g (Dietary Fiber 3g); Protein 35g **Exchanges:** 2 Starch, 1 Other Carbohydrate, ½ Vegetable, 3 Medium-Fat Meat, 1 High-Fat Meat, 3½ Fat **Carbohydrate Choices:** 3

Pasta Pairing

Serve the manicotti with favorite Mexican toppings, such as guacamole, sliced green onions, chopped tomatoes, sliced ripe olives and pickled jalapeño slices.

baked ziti with roasted tomatoes

prep time: 30 Minutes • **start to finish:** 55 Minutes • 6 servings

2½ cups uncooked ziti pasta (9 oz)

8 oz extra-lean (at least 90%) ground beef

1 large sweet onion, chopped (1 cup)

2 cloves garlic, finely chopped

1 medium zucchini, cut lengthwise in half, then cut crosswise into ¼-inch slices

1 can (15 oz) tomato sauce

1 can (14.5 oz) fire-roasted diced tomatoes, drained

2 teaspoons chopped fresh or ½ teaspoon dried oregano leaves

¼ teaspoon kosher (coarse) salt

¼ teaspoon pepper

½ cup shredded mozzarella cheese

....

Improvise

Use ground turkey or chicken in place of the ground beef, if you like.

1 Heat oven to 375°F. Spray 12x8-inch (2-quart) glass baking dish with cooking spray. Cook pasta as directed on package, omitting salt and oil and using minimum cook time; drain.

2 Meanwhile, in 12-inch nonstick skillet, cook beef, onion and garlic over medium heat 8 to 10 minutes, stirring occasionally, until beef is thoroughly cooked; drain.

3 Add zucchini to beef mixture; cook 2 minutes. Stir in tomato sauce, tomatoes, oregano, salt and pepper. Heat to boiling. Add pasta; toss to coat. Spread in baking dish.

4 Cover tightly with foil. Bake 20 minutes. Uncover; sprinkle with cheese. Bake about 5 minutes longer or until cheese is melted.

1 Serving: Calories 280; Total Fat 6g (Saturated Fat 2.5g; Trans Fat 0g); Cholesterol 0mg; Sodium 750mg; Total Carbohydrate 41g (Dietary Fiber 5g); Protein 17g **Exchanges:** 1½ Starch, ½ Other Carbohydrate, 2 Vegetable, 1 Medium-Fat Meat
Carbohydrate Choices: 3

make-ahead cheeseburger lasagna

prep time: 35 Minutes • start to finish: 10 Hours 5 Minutes • 8 servings

1½ lb lean (at least 80%) ground beef

3 tablespoons dried minced onion

1 can (15 oz) tomato sauce

1½ cups water

½ cup ketchup

1 tablespoon yellow mustard

1 egg

1 container (15 oz) ricotta cheese

2 cups shredded American-Cheddar cheese blend

12 uncooked lasagna noodles

1 cup shredded Cheddar cheese

1 cup shredded lettuce

1 medium tomato, sliced

½ cup dill pickle slices

Improvise

Although this recipe is great to make ahead, you can bake it right away, too. Just cover the dish with foil and bake as directed.

1 Spray 13x9-inch (3-quart) glass baking dish with cooking spray. In 12-inch nonstick skillet, cook beef and onion over medium-high heat 5 to 7 minutes, stirring occasionally, until beef is thoroughly cooked; drain. Stir in tomato sauce, water, ketchup and mustard. Simmer 5 minutes, stirring occasionally.

2 Meanwhile, in medium bowl, beat egg with fork or whisk. Stir in ricotta cheese and 2 cups cheese blend.

3 Spread 1 cup beef mixture in bottom of baking dish. Top with 4 uncooked noodles. Spread half of the ricotta mixture over noodles; top with 1½ cups beef mixture. Repeat layers once with 4 noodles, remaining ricotta mixture and 1½ cups beef mixture. Top with remaining 4 noodles, beef mixture and 1 cup Cheddar cheese. Cover with foil; refrigerate at least 8 hours but no longer than 24 hours.

4 Heat oven to 350°F. Bake lasagna covered 45 minutes. Uncover; bake 25 to 35 minutes longer or until bubbly. Remove from oven. Cover with foil; let stand 5 to 10 minutes before cutting.

5 Just before serving, top with lettuce, tomato and pickles. If desired, serve with additional ketchup.

1 Serving: Calories 590; Total Fat 32g (Saturated Fat 17g; Trans Fat 1g); Cholesterol 135mg; Sodium 1050mg; Total Carbohydrate 38g (Dietary Fiber 3g); Protein 39g
Exchanges: 2 Starch, ½ Other Carbohydrate, 5 Medium-Fat Meat, 1 Fat
Carbohydrate Choices: 2½

bruschetta-topped pasta and meatballs

prep time: 15 Minutes • **start to finish:** 50 Minutes • **8 servings**

- ½ cup refrigerated basil pesto (from 7-oz container)
- 1 can (15 oz) extra-thick and zesty tomato sauce
- 2 tablespoons sun-dried tomato paste (from 2.8-oz tube)
- ¼ teaspoon crushed red pepper flakes
- 1 cup water
- 1½ cups uncooked fusilli pasta (about 4½ oz)
- 26 frozen Italian meatballs (about half of 26-oz bag)
- 1 cup shredded Parmesan cheese
- 1 tablespoon butter, softened
- 2 tablespoons refrigerated basil pesto (from 7-oz container)
- 8 diagonal slices (½ inch thick) baguette French bread (from 3-inch diameter loaf)
- 8 to 10 oz cherry or grape tomatoes, halved
- 2 tablespoons shredded Parmesan cheese

1 Heat oven to 350°F. Spray 2-quart microwavable casserole with cooking spray.

2 In casserole, mix ½ cup pesto, the tomato sauce, tomato paste, pepper flakes and water. Cover with microwavable plastic wrap. Microwave on High 3 to 4 minutes or until sauce is hot. Add pasta; stir gently. Stir in meatballs and 1 cup cheese. Push any pasta that is above liquid down into liquid to cover.

3 Bake 25 minutes. Meanwhile, in small cup or bowl, mix butter and 2 tablespoons pesto. Spread mixture on each baguette slice; set aside.

4 Remove casserole from oven. Stir pasta; gently fold in tomatoes. Arrange baguette slices, overlapping if necessary, on pasta mixture to cover most of mixture. Cover loosely with foil; bake 10 minutes.

5 Uncover casserole; sprinkle with 2 tablespoons cheese. Bake about 10 minutes longer or until pasta is fork-tender.

1 Serving: Calories 540; Total Fat 30g (Saturated Fat 10g; Trans Fat 0.5g); Cholesterol 35mg; Sodium 1240mg; Total Carbohydrate 45g (Dietary Fiber 4g); Protein 23g **Exchanges:** 1 Starch, 2 Other Carbohydrate, ½ Lean Meat, 2½ Medium-Fat Meat, 3 Fat **Carbohydrate Choices:** 3

Pasta Point

You don't have to cook the pasta before adding it to this casserole. Just be sure to push any pasta below the surface of the liquid so that it gets softened during baking.

meat lover's pizza casserole

prep time: 20 Minutes • **start to finish:** 1 Hour • **8 servings**

1 package (16 oz) ziti or other tubular pasta (5 cups)

8 oz bulk Italian pork sausage

1 medium onion, chopped (½ cup)

1 medium green bell pepper, chopped (1 cup)

2 cloves garlic, finely chopped

2 cans (15 oz each) pizza sauce

8 slices bacon, crisply cooked, crumbled

½ package (3.5-oz size) sliced pepperoni

2 cups shredded Italian cheese blend

1 Heat oven to 350°F. Spray 3-quart casserole with cooking spray. Cook and drain pasta as directed on package, using minimum cook time. Return to saucepan.

2 Meanwhile, in 12-inch skillet, cook and stir sausage, onion, bell pepper and garlic over medium-high heat about 7 minutes or until sausage is no longer pink and onion is softened. Stir in pizza sauce, bacon and pepperoni.

3 Pour sausage mixture over cooked pasta; stir. Spoon half of pasta mixture (about 4 cups) into casserole. Sprinkle with 1 cup of the cheese. Spoon remaining pasta mixture on top.

4 Bake uncovered 30 minutes. Top with remaining 1 cup cheese. Bake 5 to 10 minutes longer or until hot in center and cheese is melted and bubbly.

1 Serving: Calories 540; Total Fat 21g (Saturated Fat 9g; Trans Fat 0g); Cholesterol 50mg; Sodium 1350mg; Total Carbohydrate 61g (Dietary Fiber 5g); Protein 27g **Exchanges:** 2½ Starch, 1 Other Carbohydrate, 1 Vegetable, 2½ High-Fat Meat
Carbohydrate Choices: 4

Improvise

For authentic Italian flavor, use cooked, crumbled pancetta instead of the bacon.

ravioli sausage lasagna

prep time: 20 Minutes • start to finish: 9 Hours 30 Minutes • 8 servings

1¼ lb bulk Italian pork sausage

1 jar (26 to 28 oz) tomato pasta sauce (any variety)

1 package (25 to 27.5 oz) frozen cheese-filled ravioli

2½ cups shredded mozzarella cheese (10 oz)

2 tablespoons grated Parmesan cheese

1 In 10-inch skillet, cook sausage over medium heat, stirring occasionally, until no longer pink; drain.

2 In ungreased 13x9-inch (3-quart) glass baking dish, spread ½ cup of the pasta sauce. Arrange single layer of frozen ravioli over sauce; evenly pour 1 cup pasta sauce over ravioli. Sprinkle evenly with 1½ cups sausage and 1 cup of the mozzarella cheese. Repeat layers with remaining ravioli, pasta sauce and sausage.

3 Cover tightly with foil; refrigerate at least 8 hours but no longer than 24 hours.

4 Heat oven to 350°F. Bake covered 45 minutes. Remove foil; sprinkle with remaining 1½ cups mozzarella and the Parmesan cheese. Bake about 15 minutes longer or until cheese is melted and lasagna is hot in center. Let stand 10 minutes before cutting.

1 Serving: Calories 500; Total Fat 24g (Saturated Fat 10g; Trans Fat 0g); Cholesterol 60mg; Sodium 1170mg; Total Carbohydrate 49g (Dietary Fiber 2g); Protein 23g
Exchanges: 1½ Starch, 1½ Other Carbohydrate, 2½ High-Fat Meat, 1 Fat
Carbohydrate Choices: 3

••

Pasta Point

Let pasta casseroles stand a short time after baking for easier cutting and serving.

••

Pasta Pairing

Serve with thick slices of garlic bread and a tossed green salad. If you still have room for dessert, offer scoops of raspberry and chocolate sorbet.

cheesy pizza casserole

prep time: 20 Minutes • **start to finish:** 9 Hours 40 Minutes • 6 servings

1 lb mild Italian pork sausage

2 cups water

1 can (15 oz) pizza sauce

1 can (14.5 oz) diced tomatoes with sweet onion, undrained

4 cups uncooked rotini pasta (10 oz)

1 can (2.25 oz) sliced ripe olives, drained

1½ cups shredded mozzarella or pizza cheese blend

1 In 10-inch skillet, cook sausage over medium-high heat 8 to 10 minutes, stirring frequently, until no longer pink; drain.

2 In ungreased 13x9-inch (3-quart) glass baking dish, mix water, pizza sauce and tomatoes. Stir in cooked sausage, uncooked pasta and olives (pasta should be completely covered with sauce). Cover tightly with foil; refrigerate at least 8 hours but no longer than 24 hours.

3 Heat oven to 350°F. Stir casserole; cover with foil and bake 1 hour to 1 hour 15 minutes or until bubbly.

4 Uncover baking dish; stir casserole. Sprinkle with cheese; bake uncovered 5 minutes longer or until cheese is melted.

1 Serving: Calories 500; Total Fat 22g (Saturated Fat 9g; Trans Fat 0g); Cholesterol 60mg; Sodium 1250mg; Total Carbohydrate 50g (Dietary Fiber 5g); Protein 26g **Exchanges:** 3 Starch, ½ Other Carbohydrate, 2½ High-Fat Meat **Carbohydrate Choices:** 3

••

Pasta Pairing

Olives are a nice addition to this casserole, but you can omit them for a more kid-friendly meal. Serve with warm breadsticks and a green salad.

baked ziti casserole

prep time: 20 Minutes • **start to finish:** 50 Minutes • 6 servings

1½ cups uncooked ziti pasta (5 oz)

1 lb bulk Italian pork sausage

1 pouch (9 oz) fire-roasted tomato cooking sauce or 1 cup fire-roasted tomato sauce

¼ teaspoon pepper

1 cup ricotta cheese

¼ cup grated Parmesan cheese

1 egg

1 cup shredded mozzarella cheese

Chopped fresh basil leaves, if desired

1 Heat oven to 375°F. Cook and drain pasta as directed on package.

2 Meanwhile, in 12-inch skillet, cook sausage over medium-high heat, stirring occasionally, until no longer pink; drain. Add cooking sauce, pepper and the cooked pasta; stir well.

3 In small bowl, mix ricotta cheese, Parmesan cheese and egg.

4 Spoon pasta mixture into ungreased 11x7-inch (2-quart) glass baking dish. Spoon ricotta cheese mixture on top; sprinkle with mozzarella cheese. Spray sheet of foil with cooking spray; cover baking dish with foil, sprayed side down.

5 Bake 25 to 30 minutes, removing foil for last 10 minutes of bake time, until cheese melts and mixture is hot and bubbly. Sprinkle with basil.

1 Serving: Calories 460; Total Fat 23g (Saturated Fat 11g; Trans Fat 0g); Cholesterol 100mg; Sodium 880mg; Total Carbohydrate 37g (Dietary Fiber 3g); Protein 26g **Exchanges:** 2 Starch, ½ Other Carbohydrate, ½ Vegetable, 1 Medium-Fat Meat, 1½ High-Fat Meat, 1 Fat **Carbohydrate Choices:** 2½

• •

Improvise

Instead of ricotta cheese, you can substitute ¾ cup cottage cheese and increase the Parmesan cheese to ½ cup.

For a spicy flavor kick, try using hot Italian pork sausage.

bacon-pepper mac and cheese

prep time: 25 Minutes • **start to finish:** 50 Minutes • **4 servings**

3 cups uncooked penne pasta (9 oz)

⅓ cup butter

1 medium red bell pepper, thinly sliced (about 1 cup)

4 medium green onions, sliced (¼ cup)

¼ cup all-purpose flour

½ teaspoon salt

¼ teaspoon pepper

1 teaspoon Dijon mustard

2¼ cups milk

10 slices packaged precooked bacon (from 2.2-oz package), cut into ½-inch pieces

1 cup shredded sharp Cheddar cheese

4 oz Muenster cheese, shredded (1 cup)

2 oz Gruyère cheese, shredded (½ cup)

¼ cup Italian-style bread crumbs

1 Heat oven to 350°F. Spray 2-quart casserole with cooking spray. Cook and drain pasta as directed on package, using minimum cook time.

2 Meanwhile, in 3-quart saucepan, melt butter over low heat. Reserve 1 tablespoon of the butter in small bowl. Cook bell pepper and onions in butter over medium heat 1 minute, stirring constantly. Stir in flour, salt, pepper and mustard. Cook, stirring constantly, until mixture is bubbly. Increase heat to medium-high. Gradually add milk, stirring constantly until mixture boils and thickens, about 5 minutes. Gently stir in bacon and pasta.

3 Remove from heat; stir in cheeses. Pour into casserole. Stir bread crumbs into reserved melted butter. Sprinkle over pasta mixture. Bake uncovered 20 to 25 minutes or until edges are bubbly.

1 Serving: Calories 1010; Total Fat 51g (Saturated Fat 29g; Trans Fat 1.5g); Cholesterol 145mg; Sodium 1790mg; Total Carbohydrate 91g (Dietary Fiber 5g); Protein 45g
Exchanges: 5½ Starch, ½ Other Carbohydrate, 4 High-Fat Meat, 3 Fat
Carbohydrate Choices: 6

....

Improvise

You can use elbow macaroni in place of the penne. You can also use Swiss cheese instead of the Gruyère, although Gruyère has a more pronounced nutty flavor than regular Swiss.

....

Pasta Point

Look for packages of precooked bacon near the regular bacon at your grocery store.

bacon, kale and tomato mac and cheese

prep time: 25 Minutes • **start to finish:** 1 Hour • **6 servings**

CASEROLE

- 5 slices bacon
- ¼ cup butter
- 3 tablespoons all-purpose flour
- 1 teaspoon dry mustard
- ½ teaspoon salt
- ⅛ teaspoon pepper
- 3 cups milk
- 8 oz white sharp Cheddar cheese, shredded (2 cups)
- 1½ cups uncooked elbow macaroni (6 oz)
- 1 cup finely chopped fresh kale or spinach, stems removed (about 7 oz)
- 1 can (14.5 oz) fire-roasted diced tomatoes, drained

TOPPING

- 1 tablespoon butter
- ½ cup panko crispy bread crumbs

1 Heat oven to 375°F. Spray 2-quart casserole with cooking spray. Arrange bacon between sheets of microwavable paper towels on microwavable dinner plate. Microwave on High 3 to 4 minutes or until bacon is crisp. Cool; crumble.

2 In 3-quart saucepan, melt ¼ cup butter over low heat. Stir in flour, mustard, salt and pepper. Cook over medium heat, stirring constantly, until mixture is smooth and bubbly. Remove from heat. Gradually stir in milk. Heat to boiling over medium heat, stirring constantly; boil 1 minute. Stir in cheese, ½ cup at a time, until melted. Remove from heat. Stir in uncooked macaroni. Gently stir in kale, tomatoes and bacon; pour into casserole.

3 Bake uncovered 15 minutes; stir. (If any macaroni is above surface, press down with back of spoon.) Meanwhile, in small microwavable bowl, microwave 1 tablespoon butter uncovered on High about 40 seconds or until melted. Stir in bread crumbs.

4 Sprinkle topping over macaroni mixture. Bake 12 to 17 minutes longer or until macaroni is tender when pierced with fork and topping is light golden brown. Let stand 5 minutes before serving.

1 Serving: Calories 540; Total Fat 29g (Saturated Fat 17g; Trans Fat 1g); Cholesterol 80mg; Sodium 830mg; Total Carbohydrate 47g (Dietary Fiber 2g); Protein 23g **Exchanges:** 3 Starch, ½ Vegetable, 1½ High-Fat Meat, 3 Fat **Carbohydrate Choices:** 3

Improvise

You can use an 8-ounce package of shredded cheese to save time, if you like. We prefer hand-shredded cheese for this recipe because the coating on pre-shredded cheese causes the baked casserole sauce to not be quite as smooth—but in a time crunch, pre-shredded cheese will be just fine!

Mac and Cheese Toppings

Macaroni and cheese is a favorite comfort food and is wonderful just as it is. But sometimes it's nice to add a different cheese or tasty topping for a change of pace. Here are some ideas to try.

Sprinkle on top before baking:

- Mix ½ cup fresh or dried bread crumbs with 2 tablespoons melted butter or olive oil
- ½ cup crushed plain potato chips
- ½ cup French-fried onions

Add just before removing from oven:

- ½ cup additional shredded cheese (bake 3 to 5 minutes longer or until cheese is melted)

Sprinkle on about ½ cup of any of the following after baking — or serve alongside:

- Crushed plain or flavored croutons
- Crushed crackers, flavored potato chips or snack chips
- Chopped fresh parsley or other herbs
- Sliced or cubed avocado
- Thinly sliced or chopped tomatoes
- Salsa or sour cream
- Diced bell peppers
- Sliced olives

Swap the Cheese

Use any of the following cheeses in place of all or part of the Cheddar in Macaroni and Cheese (page 35):

- Asiago or Parmesan (up to 1 cup)
- Blue or Gorgonzola, crumbled (up to 1 cup)
- Brie, crumbled (up to 1 cup)
- Cheddar (white or smoked)
- Colby
- Edam
- Fontina
- Gouda (regular or smoked)
- Gruyère or Swiss
- Havarti or Jarlsberg
- Manchego
- Monterey Jack or pepper Jack

Chopped basil

Cubed avocado

Salsa

Cheddar cheese

cheesy sausage and penne casserole

prep time: 30 Minutes • start to finish: 1 Hour • 6 servings

3 cups uncooked penne pasta (about 10 oz)

¼ cup butter

⅓ cup all-purpose flour

½ teaspoon salt

½ teaspoon Italian seasoning

¼ teaspoon pepper

2 cloves garlic, finely chopped

3 cups milk

2 cups shredded Italian cheese blend

½ cup grated Parmesan cheese

8 oz smoked sausage, sliced

¼ teaspoon Italian seasoning

1 Heat oven to 350°F. Cook and drain pasta as directed on package.

2 Meanwhile, in 3-quart saucepan, melt butter over low heat. Stir in flour, salt, ½ teaspoon Italian seasoning, the pepper and garlic. Cook over medium-low heat, stirring constantly, until mixture is smooth and bubbly; remove from heat. Stir in milk. Heat to boiling over medium-high heat, stirring constantly. Boil and stir 1 minute; remove from heat. Stir in Italian cheese blend and ¼ cup of the Parmesan cheese until melted.

3 Gently stir pasta and sausage into cheese sauce. Pour into ungreased 3-quart casserole. Sprinkle with remaining ¼ cup Parmesan cheese and ¼ teaspoon Italian seasoning. Bake uncovered about 30 minutes or until bubbly.

1 Serving: Calories 670; Total Fat 34g (Saturated Fat 18g; Trans Fat 1g); Cholesterol 90mg; Sodium 1350mg; Total Carbohydrate 62g (Dietary Fiber 3g); Protein 30g **Exchanges:** 3½ Starch, ½ Low-Fat Milk, 2½ Medium-Fat Meat, 3½ Fat **Carbohydrate Choices:** 4

Improvise

Additional pasta shapes that work in this casserole include elbow macaroni, medium shells, radiatore, rotini and cavatappi.

Cooked, smoked sausage is used in this hearty macaroni and cheese to give it a subtle smoky flavor. Reduced-fat smoked sausage, turkey sausage or kielbasa sausage works too.

ham and cheese ziti

prep time: 15 Minutes • **start to finish:** 40 Minutes • 6 servings

2½ cups uncooked ziti pasta (9 oz)

¼ cup butter

1 clove garlic, finely chopped

¼ cup all-purpose flour

½ teaspoon salt

2 cups milk

½ teaspoon Dijon mustard

2 cups shredded Colby cheese

4 oz sliced cooked deli ham, cut into thin strips

⅓ cup grated Parmesan cheese

1 Heat oven to 350°F. Cook and drain pasta as directed on package.

2 Meanwhile, in 3-quart saucepan, melt butter over low heat. Cook garlic in butter 30 seconds, stirring frequently. Stir in flour and salt. Cook over medium heat, stirring constantly, until mixture is smooth and bubbly. Gradually stir in milk. Heat to boiling, stirring constantly. Boil and stir 1 minute. Stir in mustard and Colby cheese. Cook, stirring occasionally, until cheese is melted.

3 Stir pasta and ham into cheese sauce. Pour into ungreased 2-quart casserole. Sprinkle with Parmesan cheese. Bake uncovered 20 to 25 minutes or until bubbly.

1 Serving: Calories 510; Total Fat 25g (Saturated Fat 15g; Trans Fat 0.5g); Cholesterol 75mg; Sodium 1030mg; Total Carbohydrate 46g (Dietary Fiber 2g); Protein 25g
Exchanges: 2½ Starch, ½ Low-Fat Milk, 1 Lean Meat, 1 High-Fat Meat, 2 Fat
Carbohydrate Choices: 3

Pasta Point

Make it easy! Purchase shredded cheese at the grocery store instead of shredding your own.

creamy spinach tuna casserole

prep time: 30 Minutes • **start to finish:** 55 Minutes • 8 servings

5 cups uncooked wide egg noodles (8 oz)

1 can (18 oz) creamy mushroom soup

2 cups shredded Cheddar cheese (8 oz)

1 can (12 oz) solid white tuna in water, drained

1 box (9 oz) frozen chopped spinach, thawed, squeezed to drain

½ cup milk

2 teaspoons grated lemon peel

1 can (8 oz) Pillsbury™ refrigerated crescent dinner rolls (8 rolls)

1 Heat oven to 375°F. Spray 11x7-inch (2-quart) glass baking dish with cooking spray. Cook and drain noodles as directed on package.

2 In 12-inch skillet, heat soup and 1½ cups of the cheese over medium heat until cheese is melted. Stir in cooked noodles, tuna, spinach, milk and lemon peel; heat until bubbly. Spoon mixture into casserole.

3 Unroll dough; firmly press perforations to seal. Sprinkle dough with remaining ½ cup cheese. Starting at short side, roll up dough; pinch seam to seal. Using serrated knife, cut roll into 8 slices. Place slices, cut side up, on top of tuna mixture.

4 Bake 20 to 25 minutes or until filling is bubbly and dough is deep golden brown.

1 Serving: Calories 400 (Calories from Fat 170); Total Fat 19g (Saturated Fat 10g, Trans Fat 0g); Cholesterol 65mg; Sodium 830mg; Total Carbohydrate 35g (Dietary Fiber 1g, Sugars 4g); Protein 21g **Exchanges:** 2 Starch, ½ Other Carbohydrate, 1 Very Lean Meat, 1 High-Fat Meat, 2 Fat **Carbohydrate Choices:** 2

Improvise

In place of tuna, you can use 2 cups of shredded deli rotisserie chicken. Use sharp Cheddar cheese for more cheese flavor.

tuna-alfredo casserole

prep time: 20 Minutes • **start to finish:** 50 Minutes • 6 servings

2 cups uncooked fusilli pasta (6 oz)

1 jar (16 oz) Alfredo pasta sauce

⅓ cup dry white wine or chicken broth

1 teaspoon Italian seasoning

1 teaspoon grated lemon peel

2 cans (5 oz each) solid white albacore tuna in water, drained

1 box (9 oz) frozen sugar snap peas, thawed, drained

1 jar (4.5 oz) whole mushrooms, drained

½ cup unseasoned dry bread crumbs

2 tablespoons butter, melted

1 Heat oven to 375°F. Spray 11x7-inch (2-quart) glass baking dish or 2-quart casserole with cooking spray. Cook and drain pasta as directed on package, using minimum cook time.

2 In large bowl, stir Alfredo sauce, wine, Italian seasoning, lemon peel, tuna, peas, mushrooms and pasta. Spoon into baking dish.

3 In small bowl, stir together bread crumbs and melted butter; sprinkle over mixture in baking dish.

4 Bake 25 to 30 minutes or until topping is golden brown.

1 Serving: Calories 530; Total Fat 29g (Saturated Fat 18g; Trans Fat 1g); Cholesterol 100mg; Sodium 730mg; Total Carbohydrate 41g (Dietary Fiber 3g); Protein 24g **Exchanges:** 2½ Starch, 2½ Lean Meat, 4 Fat **Carbohydrate Choices:** 3

....

Improvise

Substitute 2 cups chopped cooked chicken for the tuna, if you desire.

cheese- and vegetable-stuffed shells

prep time: 40 Minutes • **start to finish:** 1 Hour 20 Minutes • 4 servings

16 uncooked jumbo pasta shells

1 tablespoon olive or vegetable oil

1 medium onion, chopped (½ cup)

1 small bell pepper (any color), chopped (½ cup)

2 cloves garlic, finely chopped

1 small zucchini, diced (about ¾ cup)

1 can (2.25 oz) sliced ripe olives, drained

1 jar (14 to 15 oz) tomato pasta sauce

½ cup ricotta cheese

1 egg

1 cup shredded Italian cheese blend or mozzarella cheese

¼ cup grated Parmesan cheese

1 Heat oven to 350°F. Spray 11x7-inch (2-quart) glass baking dish with cooking spray. Cook and drain pasta shells as directed on package.

2 Meanwhile, in 10-inch skillet, heat oil over medium heat until hot. Cook onion, bell pepper and garlic in oil 2 to 3 minutes, stirring occasionally, until crisp-tender. Add zucchini; cook 4 minutes, stirring occasionally.

3 Stir in olives and ¼ cup of the pasta sauce. Cook, stirring frequently, until hot. Remove from heat.

4 In medium bowl, mix ricotta cheese, egg, ½ cup of the cheese blend and Parmesan cheese. Stir in zucchini mixture until well mixed. Fill each cooked pasta shell with about 2 tablespoons zucchini mixture; place filled side up in baking dish. Pour remaining pasta sauce over shells.

5 Cover with foil; bake 30 minutes. Sprinkle with remaining ½ cup cheese blend. Bake uncovered 5 to 10 minutes longer or until bubbly and cheese is melted.

1 Serving: Calories 510; Total Fat 22g (Saturated Fat 9g; Trans Fat 0g); Cholesterol 85mg; Sodium 1160mg; Total Carbohydrate 55g (Dietary Fiber 4g); Protein 23g **Exchanges:** 2 Starch, 1½ Other Carbohydrate, 1 Vegetable, 2 High-Fat Meat, 1 Fat **Carbohydrate Choices:** 3½

Pasta Point

Ricotta is a white, moist, subtly sweet cheese with a slightly grainy texture. It is a popular ingredient in many Italian dishes.

zucchini and spinach lasagna

prep time: 40 Minutes • start to finish: 9 Hours 45 Minutes • 6 servings

2 cups tomato pasta sauce

1 medium zucchini, shredded (1 cup)

1 container (12 oz) low-fat cottage cheese (1½ cups) or 1 container (15 oz) low-fat ricotta cheese

1 package (9 oz) frozen spinach, thawed, squeezed to drain well

⅓ cup grated Parmesan cheese

2 tablespoons chopped fresh or 1½ teaspoons dried oregano leaves

8 precooked lasagna noodles (shelf stable or frozen), each about 7x3 inches

1 can (4 oz) mushroom pieces and stems, drained

2 cups shredded mozzarella cheese

1 Spray 12x10-inch sheet of foil with nonstick cooking spray. In medium bowl, combine pasta sauce and zucchini; mix well. In another medium bowl, combine cottage cheese, spinach, Parmesan cheese and oregano; mix well.

2 Spread ¼ cup sauce mixture in ungreased 8-inch square (2-quart) glass baking dish. Top with 2 lasagna noodles. Spread about ½ cup sauce mixture over noodles. Drop ½ cup of spinach mixture by small spoonfuls over sauce mixture; spread carefully. Sprinkle with one-quarter of the mushrooms and ½ cup of the mozzarella cheese.

3 Repeat layers 3 more times, beginning with noodles. Cover with foil, sprayed side down; refrigerate at least 8 hours but no longer than 24 hours.

4 Heat oven to 400°F. Bake covered 45 minutes.

5 Uncover baking dish; bake 10 minutes longer or until lasagna is bubbly around edges. Let stand 10 minutes before serving.

1 Serving: Calories 350; Total Fat 13g (Saturated Fat 6g, Trans Fat 0g); Cholesterol 35mg; Sodium 930mg; Total Carbohydrate 32g (Dietary Fiber 4g); Protein 24g **Exchanges:** 2 Starch, 1 Vegetable, 1 Medium-Fat Meat, 1 High-Fat Meat **Carbohydrate Choices:** 2

Pasta Point

Look for precooked oven-ready lasagna noodles near the dry pasta in the grocery store or in the frozen pasta section. Trim the precooked lasagna noodles to fit, if necessary.

Improvise

If you prefer not to make this ahead, this recipe may be baked immediately after assembly. Cover the dish with foil and bake at 400°F for 30 minutes. Uncover the dish and continue baking about 10 minutes longer or until it is bubbly around the edges.

garden vegetable lasagna

prep time: 50 Minutes • **start to finish:** 1 Hour 55 Minutes • 8 servings

8 uncooked lasagna noodles

1 tablespoon olive or vegetable oil

1 garlic clove, minced

3 cups frozen broccoli cuts

1½ cups (about 4 oz) sliced fresh mushrooms

1 medium red, yellow or orange bell pepper, coarsely chopped (about 1 cup)

1 egg

1 container (15 oz) ricotta cheese

1 teaspoon dried Italian seasoning

1 jar (26 to 28 oz) chunky vegetable tomato pasta sauce

2 cups shredded 6-cheese Italian cheese blend

1 Cook lasagna noodles as directed on package. Drain; place in cold water to cool.

2 Meanwhile, heat oven to 350°F. In large skillet, heat oil over medium-high heat until hot. Add garlic, broccoli, mushrooms and bell pepper; cook 3 to 4 minutes, stirring frequently, until vegetables are crisp-tender. Remove from heat. If necessary, cut broccoli into smaller pieces.

3 In small bowl, beat egg with whisk. Add ricotta cheese and Italian seasoning; mix well.

4 Drain cooled lasagna noodles. Spread ½ cup of the pasta sauce in ungreased 13x9-inch (3-quart) glass baking dish. Top with 4 noodles, overlapping as necessary, half of ricotta mixture, half of cooked vegetables, half of remaining pasta sauce (about 2¼ cups) and 1 cup of the cheese blend. Repeat layers, starting with noodles.

5 Bake 45 to 50 minutes or until hot and bubbly. If cheese is getting too brown, cover baking dish loosely with foil. Let stand 15 minutes before serving.

1 Serving: Calories 410; Total Fat 19g (Saturated Fat 9g, Trans Fat 0g); Cholesterol 75mg; Sodium 660mg; Total Carbohydrate 40g (Dietary Fiber 5g); Protein 21g **Exchanges:** 2½ Starch, 1 Vegetable, ½ Medium-Fat Meat, 1 High-Fat Meat, 1½ Fat **Carbohydrate Choices:** 2½

Pasta Point

Ricotta is fresh cheese with small soft curds. Its name is Italian for "recooked." Ricotta is made by reheating the whey drained from mozzarella or provolone cheese. Ricotta's mild flavor and loose texture combine well with both sweet and savory ingredients.

Improvise

The 6-cheese Italian blend contains mozzarella, smoked provolone, Parmesan, Romano, Fontina and Asiago. You can use another combination of Italian cheeses from your refrigerator in place of the 6-cheese Italian blend if you like. Try Asiago, mozzarella, Parmesan and provolone; shred the cheeses and measure 2 cups.

roasted vegetable lasagna with goat cheese

prep time: 25 Minutes • **start to finish:** 1 Hour 10 Minutes • 8 servings

3 medium bell peppers (any color), cut into 1-inch pieces

3 medium zucchini or summer squash, cut lengthwise in half, then cut crosswise into ½-inch slices

1 medium onion, cut into 8 wedges, separated into pieces

1 package (8 oz) sliced fresh mushrooms

½ teaspoon salt

¼ teaspoon pepper

12 uncooked lasagna noodles

1 package (5 to 6 oz) chèvre (goat cheese)

1 container (7 oz) refrigerated basil pesto

2 cups tomato pasta sauce

2 cups shredded Italian cheese blend

1 Heat oven to 450°F. Spray 15x10x1-inch pan with cooking spray. In pan, arrange bell peppers, zucchini, onion and mushrooms in single layer. Spray vegetables with cooking spray; sprinkle with salt and pepper. Roast 15 to 20 minutes, turning vegetables once, until crisp-tender.

2 Meanwhile, cook and drain noodles as directed on package, using minimum cook time. In medium bowl, crumble chèvre into pesto; stir.

3 Spray 13x9-inch (3-quart) glass baking dish with cooking spray. In baking dish, spread ½ cup of the pasta sauce. Top with 3 noodles; spread with half of the pesto mixture and 2 cups of the vegetables. Add 3 noodles; layer with ¾ cup pasta sauce, 1 cup cheese blend and 2 cups vegetables. Add 3 noodles; layer with remaining pesto mixture and vegetables. Top with remaining 3 noodles; layer with remaining ¾ cup pasta sauce and 1 cup cheese blend.

4 Reduce oven temperature to 375°F. Bake 20 to 30 minutes or until hot. Let stand 10 minutes before serving.

1 Serving: Calories 520; Total Fat 26g (Saturated Fat 10g; Trans Fat 0g); Cholesterol 30mg; Sodium 990mg; Total Carbohydrate 47g (Dietary Fiber 5g); Protein 22g
Exchanges: 1½ Starch, 1 Other Carbohydrate, 2 Vegetable, 2 High-Fat Meat, 2 Fat
Carbohydrate Choices: 3

butternut squash pasta bake

prep time: 25 Minutes • **start to finish:** 50 Minutes • 6 servings

3 cups uncooked penne pasta (9 oz)

2 packages (12 oz each) frozen butternut squash

1 cup milk

1 cup chicken broth (from 32-oz carton)

2 cups shredded Italian cheese blend

¼ cup butter, cut into pieces

¼ cup pine nuts, toasted*

2 tablespoons chopped fresh sage leaves

½ teaspoon salt

¼ teaspoon pepper

Additional chopped fresh sage, if desired

1 Heat oven to 350°F. Spray 11x7-inch (2-quart) glass baking dish with cooking spray. In Dutch oven or saucepan, cook pasta as directed on package, using minimum cook time; drain and return to Dutch oven.

2 Meanwhile, cook squash in microwave as directed on package. In 3-quart saucepan, mix squash, milk, broth, 1 cup of the cheese blend and the butter. Cook over medium heat 4 to 5 minutes, stirring occasionally, until butter and cheese are melted. Remove from heat; stir in pine nuts, 2 tablespoons sage, the salt and pepper.

3 Stir squash mixture into pasta. Spoon into baking dish; sprinkle with remaining 1 cup cheese blend. Place baking dish on cookie sheet.

4 Bake uncovered 20 to 25 minutes or until lightly browned and cheese is melted. Garnish with additional sage.

*To toast pine nuts, sprinkle in ungreased skillet. Cook over medium heat 5 to 7 minutes, stirring frequently until browning begins, then stirring constantly until golden brown.

1 Serving: Calories 480; Total Fat 23g (Saturated Fat 12g; Trans Fat 0.5g); Cholesterol 55mg; Sodium 860mg; Total Carbohydrate 50g (Dietary Fiber 5g); Protein 19g
Exchanges: 3½ Starch, 1 High-Fat Meat, 2½ Fat **Carbohydrate Choices:** 3

cheesy rigatoni with eggplant sauce

prep time: 20 Minutes • start to finish: 50 Minutes • 4 servings

2½ cups uncooked rigatoni pasta (7 oz)

2 tablespoons olive oil

1 medium onion, chopped (½ cup)

1 small unpeeled eggplant, cut into ½-inch cubes (3 cups)

1 medium zucchini, cut lengthwise in half, then cut crosswise into ¼-inch slices (1½ cups)

1 can (14.5 oz) diced tomatoes with basil, garlic and oregano, undrained

1 can (8 oz) tomato sauce

1½ cups shredded mozzarella cheese

1 Heat oven to 350°F. Spray 12x8-inch (2-quart) glass baking dish with cooking spray. Cook and drain pasta as directed on package, using minimum cook time.

2 Meanwhile, in 12-inch nonstick skillet, heat oil over medium-high heat. Add onion, eggplant and zucchini; cook 5 to 7 minutes, stirring frequently, until crisp-tender. Stir in tomatoes and tomato sauce.

3 Spoon cooked pasta into baking dish. Spoon vegetable sauce over pasta.

4 Cover tightly with foil. Bake 20 minutes. Uncover; sprinkle with cheese. Bake uncovered 5 to 7 minutes longer or until cheese is melted.

1 Serving: Calories 540; Total Fat 17g (Saturated Fat 6g; Trans Fat 0g); Cholesterol 25mg; Sodium 1000mg; Total Carbohydrate 71g (Dietary Fiber 8g); Protein 25g **Exchanges:** 4 Starch, 2 Vegetable, 1 Medium-Fat Meat, 2 Fat **Carbohydrate Choices:** 5

....

Pasta Point

This dish is easily put together the night before and baked the next night for dinner. Since it will be cold, bake it about 10 minutes longer before topping with the cheese.

mushroom-fettuccine bake

prep time: 25 Minutes • **start to finish:** 55 Minutes • 8 servings

1 box (16 oz) fettuccine

3 tablespoons olive oil

1 lb assorted wild mushrooms (crimini, oyster, portabella, shiitake), sliced

1 large onion, cut into wedges (about 1½ cups)

1 teaspoon dried thyme leaves

1 teaspoon salt

¼ teaspoon pepper

2 tablespoons all-purpose flour

1½ cups vegetable broth

1½ cups heavy whipping cream

¼ cup chopped fresh parsley

4 oz chèvre (goat cheese), crumbled (1 cup)

1 cup shredded Parmesan cheese

1 Heat oven to 400°F. Spray 13x9-inch (3-quart) glass baking dish with cooking spray. Cook and drain fettuccine as directed on package.

2 Meanwhile, in 12-inch nonstick skillet, heat oil over medium-high heat. Add mushrooms, onion, thyme, salt and pepper; cook 10 minutes, stirring occasionally, until tender. Remove from heat. Stir in flour; gradually stir in broth. Heat to boiling; boil 1 minute. Remove from heat; stir in whipping cream.

3 Add fettuccine and parsley to skillet; toss. Add goat cheese; toss gently. Spoon into baking dish.

4 Cover; bake 15 minutes. Uncover; sprinkle with Parmesan cheese. Bake 10 to 15 minutes longer or until thoroughly heated and bubbly.

1 Serving: Calories 540; Total Fat 31g (Saturated Fat 16g; Trans Fat 1g); Cholesterol 115mg; Sodium 800mg; Total Carbohydrate 45g (Dietary Fiber 3g); Protein 18g **Exchanges:** 3 Starch, ½ Vegetable, 1 Medium-Fat Meat, 5 Fat **Carbohydrate Choices:** 3

Pasta Point

The goat cheese in this recipe is not meant to be melted smoothly throughout the sauce. Some of the crumbles melt, and others will surprise you when you take a bite of this casserole.

alfredo pasta pie with toasted french bread crust

prep time: 15 Minutes • **start to finish:** 40 Minutes • 6 servings

- 4 oz uncooked angel hair (capellini) pasta
- 18 slices French bread, about ¼ inch thick
- 2 tablespoons butter, softened
- ¾ cup shredded Swiss cheese
- 2 tablespoons chopped fresh or 2 teaspoons dried basil leaves
- 1 container (10 oz) refrigerated Alfredo sauce
- 3 medium plum (Roma) tomatoes, chopped (1 cup)
- 4 medium green onions, sliced (¼ cup)
- 1 tablespoon grated Romano or Parmesan cheese

1 Heat oven to 400°F. Cook and drain pasta as directed on package.

2 Meanwhile, brush bread with butter. Line bottom and side of 10-inch pie plate with bread, buttered side up, slightly overlapping slices. Bake about 10 minutes or until light brown.

3 Reduce oven temperature to 350°F. In medium bowl, mix Swiss cheese, 1 tablespoon of the basil and the Alfredo sauce. Gently stir in pasta. Spoon into baked crust.

4 In small bowl, mix tomatoes, onions and remaining 1 tablespoon basil. Sprinkle over pasta mixture; lightly press onto surface. Sprinkle with Romano cheese.

5 Bake 15 to 20 minutes or until hot. Let stand 5 minutes before cutting.

1 Serving: Calories 480; Total Fat 24g (Saturated Fat 15g; Trans Fat 1g); Cholesterol 70mg; Sodium 580mg; Total Carbohydrate 49g (Dietary Fiber 2g); Protein 16g **Exchanges:** 3 Starch, ½ Vegetable, 1 Medium-Fat Meat, 3½ Fat **Carbohydrate Choices:** 3

Pasta Pairing

This is vegetarian comfort food and a delicious way to use up leftover French bread! The bread becomes a toasted crust for this creamy pasta pie. Just add veggies or a salad for a family-pleasing dinner.

vegetable tetrazzini

prep time: 15 Minutes • **start to finish:** 45 Minutes • **6 servings**

7 oz uncooked spaghetti

2 cups vegetable broth

2 cups half-and-half

½ cup all-purpose flour

¼ cup butter

½ teaspoon salt

¼ teaspoon pepper

2 cups frozen
mixed vegetables

1 can (2.25 oz) sliced ripe
olives, drained

½ cup slivered almonds

½ cup shredded Cheddar
cheese

1 Heat oven to 350°F. Cook and drain spaghetti as directed on package. Rinse with cold water; drain.

2 In 3-quart saucepan, mix broth, half-and-half, flour, butter, salt and pepper. Heat to boiling over medium heat, stirring constantly. Boil 1 minute, stirring constantly. Stir in spaghetti, frozen vegetables and olives. In ungreased 2-quart casserole, spread mixture. Sprinkle with almonds and cheese.

3 Bake uncovered 25 to 30 minutes or until hot and bubbly.

1 Serving: Calories 490; Total Fat 26g (Saturated Fat 13g; Trans Fat 0.5g); Cholesterol 60mg; Sodium 750mg; Total Carbohydrate 50g (Dietary Fiber 4g); Protein 14g
Exchanges: 3½ Starch, 5 Fat **Carbohydrate Choices:** 3

Improvise

Less fat doesn't mean less taste! You can trim fat and calories by substituting fat-free half-and-half for the regular half-and-half, cutting the butter from ¼ cup to 2 tablespoons and using ½ cup reduced-fat Cheddar cheese.

mixed vegetable lasagna

prep time: 40 Minutes • start to finish: 2 Hours • 8 servings

1 tablespoon olive oil

4 medium green onions, sliced (¼ cup)

2 medium zucchini, shredded (about 3 cups)

2 medium carrots, shredded (about 1 cup)

1 medium dark-orange sweet potato, peeled, shredded (about 1 cup)

1 package (8 oz) sliced fresh mushrooms (about 3 cups)

2 cloves garlic, finely chopped

1 egg

1 container (15 oz) light ricotta cheese

1 cup shredded Swiss cheese

¼ cup grated Parmesan cheese

1 teaspoon dried basil leaves

1 jar (16 oz) Alfredo pasta sauce

1½ cups water

9 uncooked lasagna noodles

1 cup shredded mozzarella cheese

2 tablespoons chopped fresh parsley

1 Heat oven to 350°F. Spray 13x9-inch (3-quart) glass baking dish with cooking spray.

2 In 12-inch nonstick skillet, heat oil over medium-high heat. Add onions, zucchini, carrots, sweet potato, mushrooms and garlic; cook 6 to 8 minutes, stirring occasionally, until mushrooms are tender. Drain off any excess liquid.

3 In medium bowl, beat egg. Stir in ricotta cheese, Swiss cheese, Parmesan cheese and basil. In separate medium bowl, mix Alfredo sauce and water.

4 Arrange 3 uncooked noodles in bottom of baking dish. Top with one-third of the sauce mixture (about 1 cup), half of the ricotta mixture and half of the vegetable mixture. Repeat layers once. Top with remaining 3 noodles and remaining sauce mixture. Sprinkle with mozzarella cheese.

5 Spray sheet of foil with cooking spray; cover baking dish tightly with foil, sprayed side down. Bake 1 hour to 1 hour 10 minutes or until bubbly around edges. Sprinkle with parsley. Let stand 10 minutes before serving.

1 Serving: Calories 530; Total Fat 33g (Saturated Fat 19g; Trans Fat 1g); Cholesterol 120mg; Sodium 500mg; Total Carbohydrate 34g (Dietary Fiber 3g); Protein 25g
Exchanges: 2 Starch, 1 Vegetable, ½ Lean Meat, 2 Medium-Fat Meat, 4 Fat
Carbohydrate Choices: 2

Improvise

Assemble the lasagna up to 24 hours in advance. Cover with foil and refrigerate until ready to bake. Bake lasagna as directed, adding 5 to 10 minutes to the bake time.

moroccan spinach lasagna

prep time: 40 Minutes • **start to finish:** 1 Hour 35 Minutes • **12 servings**

9   uncooked whole wheat lasagna noodles

2   tablespoons olive oil

1   can (15 oz) chickpeas, drained, rinsed (garbanzo beans)

1   teaspoon ground cumin

¾   teaspoon paprika

¼   teaspoon ground red pepper (cayenne)

1   medium onion, chopped (½ cup)

2   cloves garlic, finely chopped

1   jar (25 oz) marinara sauce

1½   cups shredded carrots (2 medium)

1   container (15 oz) fat-free ricotta cheese

1   bag (1 lb) frozen cut leaf spinach, thawed, squeezed to drain

2   cups shredded mozzarella cheese

1 Heat oven to 350°F. Spray 13x9-inch (3-quart) glass baking dish with cooking spray. Cook and drain noodles as directed on package, omitting salt and oil and using minimum cook time. Rinse with cold water to cool. Drain well; lay noodles flat.

2 Meanwhile, in 12-inch nonstick skillet, heat oil over medium heat. Cook chickpeas, cumin, paprika and red pepper in oil 5 minutes, stirring occasionally. Add onion and garlic; cook about 3 minutes, stirring occasionally, until vegetables are crisp-tender. Stir in marinara sauce and carrots. Heat to boiling; remove from heat.

3 In medium bowl, mix ricotta cheese and spinach. Spread about ½ cup marinara sauce mixture in baking dish. Top with 3 noodles, 1½ cups sauce mixture, half of the ricotta mixture and ¾ cup of the mozzarella cheese. Repeat layers once. Top with remaining noodles, sauce mixture and mozzarella cheese.

4 Cover; bake 35 minutes. Uncover; bake 10 to 15 minutes longer or until bubbly. Let stand 5 minutes before serving.

1 Serving: Calories 290; Total Fat 9g (Saturated Fat 3g; Trans Fat 0g); Cholesterol 20mg; Sodium 560mg; Total Carbohydrate 35g (Dietary Fiber 5g); Protein 15g **Exchanges:** 1 Starch, 1 Other Carbohydrate, 1 Vegetable, 1 Very Lean Meat, ½ Medium-Fat Meat, 1 Fat **Carbohydrate Choices:** 2

Pasta Pairing

Round out this flavorful dish with a warm baguette and a green salad with light balsamic vinaigrette dressing.

spinach-stuffed manicotti with vodka cream sauce

prep time: 25 Minutes • **start to finish:** 1 Hour • 7 servings

1 box (8 oz) manicotti pasta shells (14 shells)

2 jars (25.5 oz each) garden vegetable pasta sauce

¼ cup vodka

½ cup heavy whipping cream

2 cups shredded Italian cheese blend

½ cup sun-dried tomatoes in oil, drained, chopped

1 container (15 oz) ricotta cheese

1 box (9 oz) frozen chopped spinach, thawed, squeezed to drain

2 tablespoons julienne-cut fresh basil leaves

Pasta Point

For ease when filling the manicotti shells, shape the ricotta mixture into a log with your fingers, and simply place inside the cooked shell.

1 Heat oven to 375°F. Cook and drain pasta shells as directed on package. Rinse with cool water; drain.

2 Meanwhile, in 2-quart nonreactive saucepan, heat 1 jar of pasta sauce and the vodka to boiling. Reduce heat; simmer 3 minutes, stirring occasionally. Remove from heat; stir in whipping cream. Set aside.

3 In medium bowl, mix 1 cup of the cheese blend, the sun-dried tomatoes, ricotta and spinach.

4 In ungreased 13x9-inch (3-quart) glass baking dish, spread 1 cup of the pasta sauce from second jar (save remaining sauce for another use). Fill each pasta shell with about 3 tablespoons ricotta mixture; arrange filled side up over sauce in dish. Pour vodka pasta sauce over filled shells.

5 Cover tightly with foil; bake 30 minutes or until sauce is bubbling. Uncover; sprinkle with remaining 1 cup cheese blend. Bake 5 minutes longer or until cheese is melted. Sprinkle with basil.

1 Serving: Calories 420; Total Fat 15g (Saturated Fat 7g; Trans Fat 0g); Cholesterol 35mg; Sodium 880mg; Total Carbohydrate 48g (Dietary Fiber 6g); Protein 19g **Exchanges:** 3 Starch, ½ Vegetable, 1 Medium-Fat Meat, 2 Fat **Carbohydrate Choices:** 3

Improvise

If you would like to use dry-pack sun-dried tomatoes instead of those packed in oil, just rehydrate them first by following the package directions.

roasted butternut squash–stuffed shells

prep time: 30 Minutes • start to finish: 55 Minutes • 12 servings

- 3 cups ½-inch cubes peeled butternut squash
- 1 tablespoon olive oil
- ¼ teaspoon pepper
- 24 uncooked jumbo pasta shells
- 1 cup Fiber One™ original bran cereal
- 8 oz lean Italian turkey sausage links, casings removed
- ¾ cup fat-free ricotta cheese
- ¼ cup fat-free (skim) milk
- 1 cup firmly packed fresh baby spinach leaves, chopped
- 2 tablespoons chopped fresh sage leaves
- 1 cup reduced-fat Parmesan Alfredo pasta sauce
- ⅓ cup shredded Parmesan cheese

1 Heat oven to 425°F. In medium bowl, toss squash, oil and pepper until squash is evenly coated. Spread in single layer on ungreased cookie sheet with sides. Roast uncovered 15 to 20 minutes, stirring occasionally, until squash is tender. Cool slightly. Reduce oven temperature to 350°F.

2 Meanwhile, cook pasta shells as directed on package, omitting salt and oil and using minimum cook time; drain.

3 Place cereal in resealable food-storage plastic bag; seal bag and finely crush with rolling pin or meat mallet (or finely crush in food processor). Spray 10-inch skillet with cooking spray. Crumble sausage into skillet; cook until no longer pink, stirring occasionally. Stir in cereal.

4 In large bowl, mix ricotta cheese and milk. Stir in spinach, sage, roasted squash and sausage mixture, tossing lightly to mix.

5 Spray 13x9-inch (3-quart) glass baking dish with cooking spray. Fill each cooked pasta shell with about 3 tablespoons squash mixture; place filled side up in baking dish. Drizzle Alfredo sauce over shells; sprinkle with Parmesan cheese. Cover with foil. Bake 15 minutes. Uncover; bake 5 to 10 minutes longer or until hot.

1 Serving: Calories 190; Total Fat 6g (Saturated Fat 2g; Trans Fat 0g); Cholesterol 25mg; Sodium 360mg; Total Carbohydrate 24g (Dietary Fiber 3g); Protein 10g **Exchanges:** 1½ Starch, 1 Lean Meat, ½ Fat **Carbohydrate Choices:** 1½

• •

Pasta Pairing

To balance this meal, pair the stuffed shells with a fresh green salad, and offer fruit for dessert.

minestrone casserole

prep time: 25 Minutes • start to finish: 1 Hour 15 Minutes • 6 servings

2 cups uncooked mini lasagna (mafalda) noodles (4 oz)

3 tablespoons olive oil

1 large onion, chopped (1 cup)

2 medium carrots, sliced (1 cup)

2 medium stalks celery, sliced (1 cup)

1 medium green bell pepper, chopped (1 cup)

1 medium zucchini or yellow summer squash, quartered lengthwise, then cut crosswise into slices

2 cloves garlic, finely chopped

2 cans (15 oz each) dark red kidney beans, drained, rinsed

1 can (14.5 oz) diced tomatoes with Italian herbs, undrained

½ cup finely shredded Parmesan cheese

1 teaspoon salt

¼ teaspoon pepper

¼ cup refrigerated basil pesto

1 Heat oven to 350°F. Cook and drain noodles as directed on package, using minimum cook time.

2 Meanwhile, in 10-inch skillet, heat oil over medium heat. Add onion, carrots, celery and bell pepper; cover and cook 5 to 8 minutes, stirring occasionally, until carrots are just tender. Uncover skillet; stir zucchini and garlic into vegetable mixture. Cook and stir 1 minute longer.

3 Place noodles in ungreased 2½-quart casserole. Stir in carrot mixture, beans, tomatoes, ¼ cup of the cheese, the salt, pepper and the pesto.

4 Cover; bake 40 to 50 minutes or until hot in center. Top servings with remaining cheese, 2 teaspoons each.

1 Serving: Calories 440; Total Fat 16g (Saturated Fat 4g; Trans Fat 0g); Cholesterol 10mg; Sodium 840mg; Total Carbohydrate 54g (Dietary Fiber 11g); Protein 19g **Exchanges:** 3 Starch, 2 Vegetable, 1 Lean Meat, 2 Fat **Carbohydrate Choices:** 3½

Improvise

Minestrone is a classic dish that uses what the cook has on hand. Consider using up odds and ends of pasta packages instead of the mini lasagna noodles. Just make sure that they have about the same cooking time.

four-cheese pasta bake

prep time: **25 Minutes** • start to finish: **50 Minutes** • **6 servings**

1 package (16 oz) uncooked penne pasta

½ cup butter

2 cloves garlic, finely chopped

½ cup all-purpose flour

1 teaspoon salt

4½ cups milk

1 cup shredded provolone cheese

1 cup shredded mozzarella cheese

½ cup shredded Parmesan cheese

½ cup shredded fontina cheese

⅓ cup chopped fresh parsley, if desired

1 tablespoon butter

1 cup panko crispy bread crumbs

1 Heat oven to 350°F. Spray 13x9-inch (3-quart) glass baking dish with cooking spray. Cook and drain pasta as directed on package.

2 Meanwhile, in 4-quart saucepan or Dutch oven, melt ½ cup butter over low heat. Add garlic; cook 30 seconds, stirring frequently. With whisk, stir in flour and salt until smooth. Increase heat to medium; cook, stirring constantly, until mixture is smooth and bubbly. Gradually stir in milk. Heat to boiling, stirring constantly. Boil and stir 1 minute. Stir in cheeses. Cook until melted, stirring occasionally.

3 Stir pasta and parsley into cheese sauce. Pour mixture into baking dish.

4 In 6-inch skillet, melt 1 tablespoon butter over medium-high heat. Stir in bread crumbs. Cook and stir until crumbs are golden brown. Sprinkle over pasta mixture.

5 Bake uncovered 20 to 25 minutes or until bubbly.

1 Serving: Calories 850; Total Fat 39g (Saturated Fat 23g; Trans Fat 1g); Cholesterol 100mg; Sodium 1390mg; Total Carbohydrate 91g (Dietary Fiber 4g); Protein 35g
Exchanges: 5 Starch, 1 Other Carbohydrate, 3 High-Fat Meat, 2 Fat
Carbohydrate Choices: 6

Improvise

Panko bread crumbs are Japanese-style bread crumbs that have a coarser texture and make for a much lighter and crunchier casserole topping. Regular dry bread crumbs will also work, but you may want to use half the amount.

The four cheeses in this recipe complement each other, but you can easily use any combination of shredded cheese that you prefer. And check the pantry for other tubular pastas that can be used for the penne.

Metric Conversion Guide

VOLUME

U.S. Units	Canadian Metric	Australian Metric
¼ teaspoon	1 mL	1 ml
½ teaspoon	2 mL	2 ml
1 teaspoon	5 mL	5 ml
1 tablespoon	15 mL	20 ml
¼ cup	50 mL	60 ml
⅓ cup	75 mL	80 ml
½ cup	125 mL	125 ml
⅔ cup	150 mL	170 ml
¾ cup	175 mL	190 ml
1 cup	250 mL	250 ml
1 quart	1 liter	1 liter
1½ quarts	1.5 liters	1.5 liters
2 quarts	2 liters	2 liters
2½ quarts	2.5 liters	2.5 liters
3 quarts	3 liters	3 liters
4 quarts	4 liters	4 liters

WEIGHT

U.S. Units	Canadian Metric	Australian Metric
1 ounce	30 grams	30 grams
2 ounces	55 grams	60 grams
3 ounces	85 grams	90 grams
4 ounces (¼ pound)	115 grams	125 grams
8 ounces (½ pound)	225 grams	225 grams
16 ounces (1 pound)	455 grams	500 grams
1 pound	455 grams	0.5 kilogram

MEASUREMENTS

Inches	Centimeters
1	2.5
2	5.0
3	7.5
4	10.0
5	12.5
6	15.0
7	17.5
8	20.5
9	23.0
10	25.5
11	28.0
12	30.5
13	33.0

TEMPERATURES

Fahrenheit	Celsius
32°	0°
212°	100°
250°	120°
275°	140°
300°	150°
325°	160°
350°	180°
375°	190°
400°	200°
425°	220°
450°	230°
475°	240°
500°	260°

Note: The recipes in this cookbook have not been developed or tested using metric measures. When converting recipes to metric, some variations in quality may be noted.

index

Recipe Testing and Calculating Nutrition Information

Recipe Testing:

- Large eggs and 2% milk were used unless otherwise indicated.

- Fat-free, low-fat, low-sodium or lite products were not used unless indicated.

- No nonstick cookware and bakeware were used unless otherwise indicated. No dark-colored, black or insulated bakeware was used.

- When a pan is specified, a metal pan was used; a baking dish or pie plate means ovenproof glass was used.

- An electric hand mixer was used for mixing only when mixer speeds are specified.

Calculating Nutrition:

- The first ingredient was used wherever a choice is given, such as ⅓ cup sour cream or plain yogurt.

- The first amount was used wherever a range is given, such as 3- to 3½-pound whole chicken.

- The first serving number was used wherever a range is given, such as 4 to 6 servings.

- "If desired" ingredients were not included.

- Only the amount of a marinade or frying oil that is absorbed was included.